CATHOLICS IN NEW YORK

SOCIETY, CULTURE, AND POLITICS, 1808–1946

CATHOLICS IN NEW YORK

SOCIETY, CULTURE, AND POLITICS
1808–1946

EDITED BY **TERRY GOLWAY**

FORDHAM UNIVERSITY PRESS
MUSEUM OF THE CITY OF NEW YORK

NEW YORK, 2008

Fordham University Press
New York
www.fordhampress.com

Museum of the City of New York
1220 Fifth Avenue
New York, NY 10029
(212) 534-1672
www.mcny.org

10 9 8 7 6 5 4 3 2 1

ISBN 978-08232-2904-8

DESIGN
HvADesign
Henk van Assen with Amanda Bowers and Yuko Kawashimo

Printed in China by Four Colour Imports, Ltd.

"Life of The Party" is excerpted from *Looking for Jimmy: A Search for Irish
America* by Peter Quinn, published by Overlook Press, Woodstock & New
York, 2007. © Peter Quinn. Reprinted by permission of the publisher.

"A New Mission: Cardinal Spellman and New York's Puerto Ricans" is
adapted from *Latinos and the New Immigrant Church* by David A. Badillo
published by The Johns Hopkins University Press, Baltimore, 2006
© The Johns Hopkins University Press. Reprinted by permission
of the publisher.

COVER ILLUSTRATION
Saint Patrick's Cathedral, Easter, 1941
Museum of the City of New York, gift of
the Department of Local Government,
Public Record Office of South Australia,
90.28.52

TITLE PAGE ILLUSTRATION
Sunday Morning in Fifth Avenue, New York,
after 1905, published by Success Postal
Card Co., New York
Museum of the City of New York, Print
Archive, gift of Mrs. John J. Meralla

ABOUT THE MUSEUM OF THE CITY OF NEW YORK

The Museum of the City of New York explores the past, present, and future of New York City and celebrates its heritage of diversity, opportunity, and perpetual transformation. Founded in 1923 as a private, non-profit corporation, the Museum serves the people of New York and visitors from across the country and around the world through exhibitions, collections, publications, and school and public programs.

CONTENTS

DIRECTOR'S FOREWORD   8
Susan Henshaw Jones

INTRODUCTION   11
Terry Golway

CATHOLIC NEW YORKERS:
FAMILY, PARISH, & COMMUNITY

Confessions of A 'Retired' Catholic   23
Pete Hamill

A SEPARATE FEAST
THE ITALIAN INFLUENCE ON CATHOLIC NEW YORK   27
Mary Elizabeth Brown

A PEOPLE SET APART
THE CHURCH GROWS IN BROOKLYN...AND QUEENS   41
Patrick J. McNamara

ST. BRIGID'S PARISH
A PILGRIM CHURCH FOR AN IMMIGRANT PEOPLE   55
David Gibson

FROM SERFDOM TO FREEDOM
POLISH CATHOLICS FIND A REFUGE   69
Alex Storozynski

BUILDING CATHOLIC NEW YORK:
INSTITUTIONS AND ORGANIZATIONS

The Sweetness of a Sunday Gathering
Mother Frances Xavier Cabrini   81

SAVING GRACE
THE EMIGRANT SAVINGS BANK AND ITS DEPOSITORS   83
Tyler Anbinder

APART AND AMONG
SISTERS IN THE LIVES OF CATHOLIC NEW YORKERS   95
Bernadette McCauley

BRIDGING THE RACIAL GAP
JOHN LAFARGE AND THE CATHOLIC INTERRACIAL COUNCIL   109
James Thomas Keane, S.J.

SANCTIFIED LIVES   119

PUBLIC FACES:
CATHOLICS IN LABOR AND POLITICS

Life of the Party   127
Peter Quinn

FAITH, POWER, AND IDENTITY
CATHOLICS IN NEW YORK POLITICS   133
Salvatore J. LaGumina

SOGGARTH AROON
THE RISE AND FALL OF REV. EDWARD MCGLYNN   147
Edward T. O'Donnell

ON THE CATHOLIC WATERFRONT
STRUGGLING FOR POWER, OPPORTUNITY, AND JUSTICE   163
James T. Fisher

AN AFTERWORD:
THE NEW CATHOLIC NEW YORK

Spanish Harlem Welcomes an Irishman
William Donohue   177

A NEW MISSION
CARDINAL SPELLMAN AND NEW YORK'S PUERTO RICANS   181
David A. Badillo

GREEN GRASS, CAPE CODS, AND
SUBURBAN CATHOLICISM   189
Dan Barry

Contributor Biographies   199

Image Credits   200

Index   203

CATHOLICS IN NEW YORK
SOCIETY, CULTURE, AND POLITICS, 1808–1946

Catholics have been a part of the great mosaic of the city since the 17th century. Once a suppressed outsiders' faith, Catholicism became the region's single largest Christian denomination by the mid 19th century, a growth fueled largely by immigration. The single Manhattan parish of some two hundred communicants of 1785 had become 446 parishes within the five boroughs by the early 1990s, serving the 42% of New Yorkers who identified themselves as Roman Catholic.

This publication explores the threads that weave through the Catholic experience in New York. It begins with family, parish, and community, then moves outward into the workplace, civic and political mobilization, and the collective building of educational, health, and welfare institutions untainted by anti-Catholic sentiment. It brings the story to 1946, the year that the implementation of the GI Bill made it possible for returning veterans to go to college and graduate school, paving the way for them to move their families out of the old neighborhoods to the growing suburbs. Catholic neighborhoods and parishes throughout the five boroughs were repopulated in part by a new, even more diverse group of arrivals from around the world, as the epilogue documents.

This volume is published in conjunction with the exhibition *Catholics in New York, 1808–1946*, presented at the Museum of the City of New York on the occasion of the 200th anniversary of the formation of the Roman Catholic Archdiocese of New York. At the Archdiocese of New York, Cardinal Edward Egan graciously gave his cooperation to this undertaking, as did Bishop Nicholas DiMarzio at the Diocese of Brooklyn.

I am particularly grateful to the many people who have made the exhibition and the publication possible. Special thanks go to the supporters of this ambitious project. Seed money for *Catholics in New York* came from Russell L. Carson. Lead funding came from the Homeland Foundation, and we are particularly grateful to foundation president E. Lisk Wyckoff, Jr. Important additional support came from Emigrant Savings Bank, Adrian and Jessie Archbold Charitable Trust, Jennifer and James Cacioppo, Mrs. John L. Dowling, Paula and Thomas McInerney, Thomas C. Quick, Diane and James E. Quinn, Mr. and Mrs. James E. Buckman, Catholic Health Services of Long Island, F. J. Sciame Construction Company, Paul Guarner, Thomas S. Murphy, Julia V. Shea, Martin McLaughlin, Marie and William Powers Charitable Trust, Terence S. and Emily Souvaine Meehan, Charles Millard, Carrol A. Muccia Jr., William C. Dowling Jr. Foundation, William H. Sadlier, Inc., William M. and Miriam F. Meehan Foundation, and Jane B. and Ralph A. O'Connell. Other donors include

Catherine L. Murray, Barbara and Benjamin Denihan, Mrs. Miriam K. Moran, Arnhold and S. Bleichroeder Holdings, Inc., John M. Callagy, John V. Connorton, Jr., Convent of the Sacred Heart, Angela B. Dinger, Peter M. Flanigan, Jeffrey J. Hodgman in honor of Julia Shea, Ladies of Charity, Marymount School of New York, Edward T. Mohylowski, Emily K. Rafferty, Mr. and Mrs. Alfred E. Smith IV, and an anonymous gift.

The project would never have come to fruition without the guidance of many generous individuals. The idea of the exhibition originated with Jane B. O'Connell, and her energy and commitment kept the project moving forward. She co-chaired the Exhibition Committee with James E. Quinn, the Museum's Vice Chair, working closely with Helen T. Lowe, Julia V. Shea, and Angela B. Dinger. Together, they helped to lead a distinguished group that included James E. Buckman, James Cacioppo, Russell L. Carson, John V. Connorton, Jr., Mrs. John L. Dowling, Paul Guarner, Pete Hamill, Frank Macchiarola, Myra and Arthur J. Mahon, Howard Milstein, Edward T. Mohylowski, Thomas S. Murphy, Rev. Joseph A. O'Hare, S.J., Thomas C. Quick, Hon. Christine C. Quinn, Hon. Domenic M. Recchia, Jr., Frank J. Sciame, Alfred E. Smith IV, and E. Lisk Wyckoff, Jr. Our gratitude also goes to Sister Eileen Clifford, Dr. Catherine Hickey, and their colleagues at the Archdiocese of New York, as well as members of the staff of the Roman Catholic Diocese of Brooklyn, who have likewise been generous with their time and knowledge as the project developed. The scholarly advisory committee, including Tyler Anbinder, Mary Elizabeth Brown, Bernadette McCauley, Patrick J. McNamara, Robert A. Slayton, and Terry Golway gave invaluable guidance as the project developed. I thank them all.

This volume was the product of many hands. As editor, Terry Golway shaped the project and ably marshaled the many generous contributing authors. The Museum's senior curatorial associate, Autumn Nyiri, provided editorial support and oversaw myriad details, with the help of curatorial assistant Elizabeth Compa. Deborah Dependahl Waters, Senior Curator, who organized the exhibition, provided careful editorial guidance, along with Deputy Director and Chief Curator Sarah M. Henry. We are fortunate to have worked with a skillful design team, led by Henk Van Assen, who provided graphic design for the book. Finally, we are grateful to Robert Oppedisano and his colleagues at Fordham University Press for helping to bring this important publication project to fruition.

Susan Henshaw Jones
President and Director

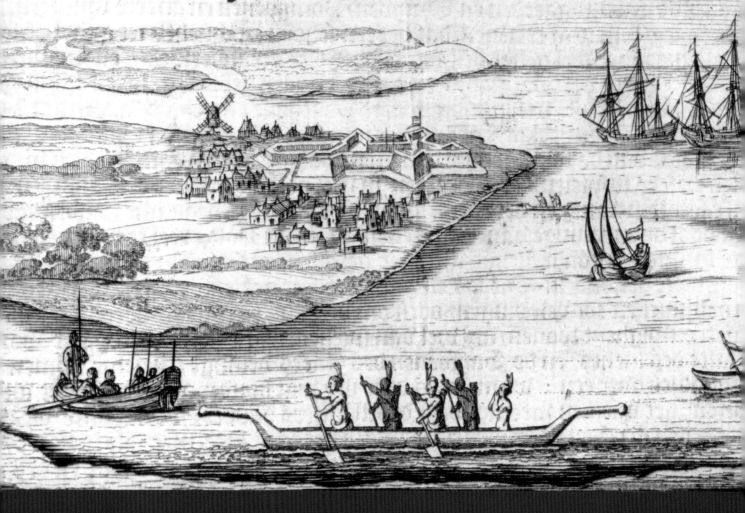

t' Fort nieúw Amsterdam op de Manhatans

INTRODUCTION

When a Jesuit missionary named Isaac Jogues visited the Dutch colony of New Amsterdam in 1643, the number of Catholics on Manhattan Island could be counted on one hand—with fingers to spare. There were, he said, just two Catholics in the settlement, a woman from Portugal and a young fellow of Irish descent who had made his way north from Maryland.

The colony's director-general, William Kieft, told Father Jogues that New Amsterdam's 400 or so residents spoke 18 languages. The town—more like a crude branch office of the Dutch West India Company—was diverse even then, with a mixture of northern and southern Europeans, Asians, South Americans, and North Africans.

By any measure, though, Catholics were as exotic as they come. The Dutch, English, and Germans in New Amsterdam were Protestants at a time when differences among Christians meant a great deal to Europeans, whether in the Old World or the New. Catholics were regarded with suspicion that easily led to open hostility. In 1700, less than 30 years after the British acquired New Amsterdam from the Dutch permanently and renamed it New York, Catholic priests were declared to be a threat to public order and were barred from the colony. At the time, there were no more than a dozen or so Catholics in New York.

By the turn of the next century, the number of Catholics in the growing city was large enough to justify the opening of a Catholic school. And when the 19th century gave way to the 20th, Catholics in New York numbered more than a million, thanks to the extraordinary

BOTTOM LEFT

Bronze medal honoring St. Isaac Jogues,
Medallic Art Co., New York, 1939
St. Isaac Jogues, a French Jesuit missionary,
visited New Netherland in 1643.

BOTTOM RIGHT

Most Reverend John Hughes, D.D., c. 1850, engraving
Archbishop John Hughes (1797–1864) defended
Catholic values in an often hostile city.

TOP LEFT

Silver beaker engraved by Joseph Leddel,
New York, 1750
Anti-Catholicism in colonial New York had its
roots in the controversies of Europe, expressed
here in a cartoon linking the Devil, the Pope,
and the Young Pretender to the British throne
Bonnie Prince Charlie (Charles Edward Stuart).

TOP RIGHT

Frontispiece to *The Wide-Awake Gift:*
***A Know-Nothing Token For 1855* edited by**
"One of 'Em," drawing by John Chester
Buttre, New York: J. C. Derby, 1855
Anti-Catholic nativists, nicknamed "Know-
Nothings," moved from secret societies into
open political activity in 1854–1855.

PAGE 10

T' Fort nieuw Amsterdam op de Manhatans
[The Hartgers View], date depicted c. 1626–
1628, engraving from *Beschrijvinghe van*
Virginia, Nieuw Nederlandt/Nieuw Engelandt,
Amsterdam: Joost Hartgers, 1651 (detail)
Dutch New Amsterdam with the fort at its
heart was a frontier trading center.

influx of immigrants from Ireland, Germany, Italy, and Poland. Today, in the opening years of the new millennium, New York once again is reinventing itself with a new wave of immigration. And like the immigrants of old, many of the newcomers, particularly those from South and Central America, Nigeria, and the Philippines, are Catholics.

What, then, does it mean to be a Catholic in New York? As this collection of essays will demonstrate, the answer depends on context, for being a New York Catholic has never been a simple matter. Nativists, who helped elect one mayor in antebellum New York, believed that the Catholics who were pouring into the city in the 1830s, 1840s, and 1850s were a monolith that took its political, cultural, and spiritual cues from the Pope. That perception has been hard for Catholic New Yorkers to shake, despite a wealth of evidence showing that while New York Catholics share a tradition of faith—no small matter—they have disagreed among themselves about nearly everything else. Including, or especially, politics.

Today, we call this diversity, and we like it.

The Museum of the City of New York's exhibition *Catholics in New York, 1808 to 1946* and this collection of essays, published in tandem with the exhibition, ought to demonstrate once and for all that only a brave soul would dare speak of an entity called Catholic New York. Existing under that expansive label are liberals and conservatives and the apathetic; civil servants and chief executive officers; clergy and the laity; rich, poor, and those in the middle; and the speakers of dozens of languages.

It has always been so. It surely will remain so, as old Irish and Italian parishes in Queens and the Bronx make room for new parishioners from Manila or Mexico City, as Poles in Greenpoint share space in the pews with the bohemian children of middle-class Catholics, as the churches of suburban Staten Island are transformed by the energy and faith of immigrants from West Africa.

New York's new Catholics are writing a story that a second generation, or even a third, will chronicle decades from now. We don't know now how that story will turn out. But we do know that something extraordinary began around 1800, when Catholics in New York began to have a real presence in the city, and that the story changed, abruptly and irretrievably, after World War II. And so the heart of the exhibition is centered on the foundation, growth, and prosperity of New York's older Catholic communities from the early 19th century to the middle of the 20th. This collection of essays retains that focus, although several writers have taken their topics closer to the turn of the millennium.

For purposes of broad generalization, what can we say about Catholics in New York without prompting fierce debate among language groups, ethnicities, political partisans, parish societies, and religious orders?

13

Surely one characteristic seems obvious: Catholics in New York have been and are, well, *Catholics*. They may have been converts, as were two extraordinary New York women, Dorothy Day and Elizabeth Ann Seton; they may regard themselves as "retired Catholics," as Pete Hamill does in his essay here; or they may disagree with the Church's political pronouncements, as thousands of Irish Americans did, publicly and loudly, in the turmoil of Gilded Age New York. But whatever their status, whatever their political views, wherever they were born, however early or late they were received into the Church, Catholics in New York shared and continue to share a common heritage of faith. In the following pages, Mary Elizabeth Brown and Alex Storozynski tell the story of two ethnic groups, Italians and Poles, who challenged the predominately Irish hierarchy with demands for priests who spoke the language of their respective homelands. But whatever their tongue, Catholics in New York were reared in the common language of the Mass, the sacraments, the symbols of their faith, and the belief in redemption. That language is not so easily forgotten, even among those who have not heard it in years. In his essay, Pete Hamill gratefully acknowledges the gift of that language, which retains its power even if it has, in his case, fallen into disuse.

Another generalization seems indisputable regardless of century, ethnicity, or political belief: Catholicism in New York is defined by the searing experience of anti-Catholicism, particularly the nativist backlash of the mid 19th century and its early 20th-century echoes in the hate-mongering of the Ku Klux Klan.

It is hard to think of Catholics in New York as a minority group, at least as we understand the phrase today. Until the wave of Latino immigrants arrived in recent decades, Catholics in New York were overwhelmingly white. But in an antebellum New York, proud of its Protestant roots and heritage, Catholics were a minority in every sense of the word, and were often reminded of their status. As Salvatore A. LaGumina points out in his essay on Catholic political and civic life, New York elected an avowedly nativist mayor who ran on explicitly anti-immigrant, anti-Catholic platforms in the 1840s—even before the great wave of poor Irish Catholics landed on South Street after escaping famine in their homeland.

The voice of defiance and the source of protection for New York Catholics, most of whom were Irish or German in the middle of the 19th century, was an Irish immigrant who toiled as a gardener and laborer before joining the priesthood. His name was John Hughes, and he served as bishop of New York from 1842 until his death in 1864. A man who never backed down from a fight, who saw himself as the defender of Catholic values in a hostile city, John Hughes came to believe that Catholics were better served by building walls rather than bridges. It is an unfashionable sentiment today; however, in Hughes's time, he and his allies believed they had no choice. But contributor Edward T. O'Donnell, in his essay on Father Edward McGlynn, notes that some American clerics were skeptical of Hughes's vision, insisting that Catholics ought to join the mainstream rather than build separate schools, hospitals, universities, orphanages, and other institutions.

TOP
**Cardinal Hayes laying the corner-
stone of Cathedral High School,
October 28, 1925**
The Catholic educational network
included high schools. This school
for girls, begun in 1905, was located
at the corner of Lexington Avenue
and 51st Street.

BOTTOM
**Our Lady of Peace Nursery,
Brooklyn, 1944**
Women religious were often
the public face of the Church.

**Corpus Christi procession, Wyckoff
Heights, Brooklyn, c. 1940**
Annual *Corpus Christi* processions expose
the Holy Eucharist to the community
beyond church walls.

Hughes and his allies won that tumultuous battle. Irish-Catholic self-segregation manifested itself not only in a social service and educational network, but even in finance. As contributor Tyler Andbinder writes, the Emigrant Industrial Savings Bank was founded to serve immigrant Catholics in New York. Today's New York has been shaped, in part, by John Hughes's vision of Catholic separatism. The Church's welfare and learning institutions have served hundreds of thousands of New Yorkers, including many non-Catholics. They also offered an extraordinary opportunity for Catholic women to become managers, administrators, and executives. These institutions, the building blocks of Catholic New York, were the special sphere of nuns. They staffed the schools, served as nurses in hospitals, nurtured orphans—and they ran the institutions that served the poor, the ill, and the children. What's more, they often were the public face of the Church. "Sisterhoods carefully cultivated close relationships with the Catholic laity of all classes, and those relationships facilitated their work," writes contributor Bernadette McCauley in her essay on nuns.

The legacy of Hughes's two-fisted defensiveness is evident in the city's separate Catholic sphere of schools, hospitals, and even, to an extent, the parish boundaries that superseded—for many New York Catholics—the boundaries of neighborhoods. But it can be measured in a more intangible way as well: Patrick J. McNamara, in his essay on the Diocese of Brooklyn, notes that Dorothy Day believed many New York Catholics had a permanent chip on their shoulders, seemingly ever-ready to be assailed by hostile anti-Catholics, even long after the nativist gangs of New York became mere material for Hollywood.

Speaking of Hollywood, James Fisher brings a touch of cinematic drama to this collection in his essay on the Catholic presence on New York's waterfront. Fisher, who has studied the waterfront extensively in preparation for a forthcoming book on the subject, provides the real-life background to the classic film *On the Waterfront* as he examines the role Catholic dockworkers, union leaders, managers, and priests played in the struggle to bring the Church's teachings on social justice to one of the city's toughest neighborhoods, the West Side piers.

Following in the spirit of John Hughes, Catholics in New York carved out their separate lives—centered on feast days, baptisms, weddings, and wakes—and identified themselves by their parish rather than by their neighborhood. Their rise to power and influence reached its climax after the cities of New York and Brooklyn were joined in 1898, as Catholics—most of them Irish—came to dominate city politics. In an essay about his politically active father, contributor Peter Quinn reminds us of a time when Catholic politicians helped to redefine the relationships between local neighborhoods and City Hall. But even in public life, it was futile to think of a monolithic Catholic New York position or view. Catholics like Alfred E. Smith and Charles Francis Murphy were mainstream Democrats who brought reform to New York in the 1920s. Other Catholics, such as Congressman Vito Marcantonio, were avowed leftists, and another, Elizabeth Gurley Flynn, became head of the U.S. Communist Party. Dorothy Day was a pacifist even during World War II. Father John LaFarge, a Jesuit who edited the order's magazine, *America*, was a passionate advocate for civil rights who challenged New York's white Catholics to examine their prejudices, as contributor James Keane notes in an essay on LaFarge and the Catholic Interracial Council.

Diversity of political belief reflected the diversity of experience among New York's Catholics. Contributor David Gibson examines the ways in which a single, venerable parish, St. Brigid's in the East Village, reflected the demographic, sociological, and economic changes that were a constant presence in Catholic New York. Founded by immigrants who fled starving Ireland in the mid 19th century, St. Brigid's changed as the East Village changed, until, that is, the old church could change no more. A similar transformation was under-way in East Harlem in the early 1970s, when essayist William Donohue was a young teacher in St. Lucy's parish school on East 104th Street. An Irish-American graduate student and an Air Force veteran, Donohue quickly realized that he had much to learn from his African-American and Puerto Rican students.

The end of World War II brought change to New York and to cities around the country. Highways cut through the Bronx and Brooklyn, directing residents to new lives where they could build churches with parking lots and play CYO basketball in gyms with bleacher seats and locker rooms. The Catholic experience, and every other experience, was transformed when the GIs came marching home. Many of them kept marching, north to the Hudson Valley, west to New Jersey, or east to Long Island, where the family of essayist Dan Barry settled and helped create new communities of faith.

For many Catholics of European descent, a golden age passed with the mass movement out of New York City. In the coming decades, inner city churches and schools would close, and Catholics would continue to drift away from the old neighborhood, the old parish, the old political party. The face of New York Catholicism would change; its voice would begin to lose the cadences of Dublin, Naples, and Krakow. In their place, the accents of Santo Domingo, San Juan, and São Paulo became the dominant Catholic immigrant voice of New York.

That transformation is a story for another time, for it is still unfolding. For us, today, the time has come to assess yesterday's Catholics, to revel in their successes, to puzzle over their failings, and to educate ourselves in the many faces and distinct voices of New York Catholicism.

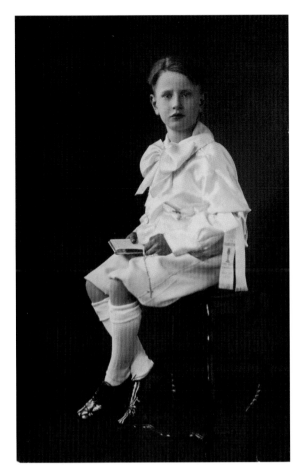

TOP LEFT
First Communion portrait of Lawrence
Colbert, 1923

TOP RIGHT
First Communion portrait of Rose Cascio,
c. 1915
New York Catholics share the common
language of their faith and its sacraments,
including First Communion.

BOTTOM
Spanish-speaking worshippers at
Our Lady of Montserrat Chapel,
Brooklyn, April 21, 1957

CATHOLIC NEW YORK: FAMILY, PARISH & COMMUNITY

William and Anne Hamill with baby Pete, 1935

Confessions of A "Retired" Catholic

I'm the oldest of seven children of Catholic immigrants from Belfast in Northern Ireland. In many ways, that accident of birth shaped my life.

My father was 20 when he arrived in Boston in 1923 and found himself two days later in the furnished room of a brother who lived in Bay Ridge. Behind him were the endless bigotries of Belfast, the snarling, invincible religious quarrels of the 17th century, the iron certainties of class, the strong Catholic belief that the deck was stacked against him and all the other Catholics of that northern province. In his late teens, he pledged allegiance to *Sinn Fein*, which meant "ourselves alone." If the Orange mobs came with guns, he was among many who were prepared to shoot back. When Michael Collins was assassinated by other Irishmen in 1922, he decided it was time to leave. He reached Brooklyn on the 4th of July. He never wanted to leave.

It took my mother a while longer. She was an orphan who had just turned 19 when she sailed past the Statue of Liberty into the greatest city in the world. She arrived with perfect Irish timing on the day the stock market crashed in 1929. In the harbor, she could see the Brooklyn waterfront, where her father, an engineer named Peter Devlin, had been killed in an accident in 1916. She was then five years old. After her father was buried in Queens, her mother took her and her brother back to Ireland, moving through the dangerous Atlantic, busy with German submarines, to seek the bitter consolations of home. When her mother died in 1928, she knew she was going back to New York.

Their American lives were not easy. My father, Billy Hamill, lost his left leg in 1927, when he was kicked too hard in a soccer game in the immigrant leagues; gangrene set in, and there was not yet penicillin, so he was left to the cure of the saw. My mother worked as a domestic, as a nanny, as a clerk at Wanamaker's. She and Billy Hamill met at a dance at Webster Hall in 1934. A dance! She saw him sitting in a pool of loneliness against a wall of the dance hall. She asked him to dance. He said he couldn't dance, without mentioning his wooden leg. "Och," she said, "neither can I." And took his hand.

And so they started "going around," as they said, Billy Hamill of Leeson Street and Anne Devlin of the Short Strand. Both now from Brooklyn forever. They married in a Catholic church and began to make their American family. They brought up all of us as Catholics, of course, and this was not adherence to empty ritual or what the great Irish Protestant poet Derek Mahon once called "pious baloney." It wasn't even out of some need to create a fortress against others, as it would have been in Belfast. It was their own way to becoming American. That is, it was a choice. They lived their Catholic lives as if there could be no other way to live.

But they were already shaped, as they in turn would shape me, my brothers, my sister. They had learned some hard lessons in Ireland. And so, in their different ways, they were determined never to do to others what had been done to them in Belfast. They would never have used a glib blur of a word like liberal to describe themselves. But they had Italian friends and Jewish friends, and they went to one another's birthday parties and family weddings and, yes, to funerals. Once, in a bar called Rattigan's, when some fool called one of my father's friends a "kike," my father leveled him with a header, as he had done so often when the target was a soccer ball. In different ways, they instructed all of their American children about the evils of bigotry. They joined an organization called Belfast United, made of immigrant Catholics and Protestants, and my mother marched with them in every St. Patrick's Day parade until the group died of old age. My father, of course, could not march. But he joined them later to celebrate. This was not Belfast. This was New York.

Most moral instruction came from my mother. She was the more devout Catholic, more articulate than my father, better educated (he had only finished the eighth grade in Belfast), full of a greater sense of the wonders of the New York world. In the hardest times, when there was never enough money, she never sought welfare; she prayed. And worked. She was always hurrying off to a part-time job, as a nurse's aide at Methodist Hospital, as a cashier at the RKO Prospect. Hurrying. Laughing.

My father's style was pure Belfast, best expressed in the title of a poem by Seamus Heaney called "Whatever You Say, Say Nothing." In Belfast, if you said the wrong thing, you could be shot dead. In his American life, Billy Hamill almost always expressed himself through songs, holding a glass at a bar, singing old music hall songs and rebel songs and sad ballads of the place left behind. When I went with him to church, he was largely silent, never singing the Latin hymns, and seldom the hymns in English.

But he was there. As a Catholic. Imperfect, capable of sin, needing forgiveness. And on the way home, he talked of Jackie Robinson, for the sports pages of the *Daily News* had most truly made him an American. He was angry about racism. He cheered when Roy Campanella doubled with men on base. And he was a Catholic until he died at 80. In our tenement kitchen, there were two pictures that represented what an academic might describe as a "belief system." One was of Jesus of Nazareth, his bleeding heart exposed, nail holes in his hands. The other was of Franklin D. Roosevelt. During the war, when I was seven, eight, nine, I was convinced that the voice of God must sound like FDR. And surely God must believe in the things my parents believed in: paying your debts, being kind to the unfortunate, avoiding cruelty, joining unions, and voting the straight ticket. Above all, avoiding the sins of pride or self-pity.

They also placed me in a Catholic grammar school named Holy Name, in nearby Windsor Terrace, and I went on to a Jesuit high school

named Regis on 84th Street near Park Avenue. Both codified the moral lessons of my parents and infused me with a way of seeing the world, along with work habits, and curiosity about life itself and tolerance about the many ways that others chose to live. I never graduated from Regis, but the Jesuits had an enduring effect upon me, one I didn't clearly understand until I'd actually lived a life. Their demands for excellence, for exactitude, for alertness, for a certain modesty, and (oddly) for doubt, shaped my adult life. In a narrower context, the rhythms of Latin remain part of my writing style. More important, I still feel the presence of a Secret Jesuit leaning over my shoulder, whispering: "Not good enough, pal."

We have all learned that there are many ways to be a New Yorker, or an American, or a man or woman. Even for those Catholics who do not practice anymore, who have lost religious faith, there are also many ways to be Catholic. The actor Peter O'Toole once said to me: "There is no such thing as an ex-Catholic. But there are many retired Catholics." And laughed out loud. Certainly, some of those retirees (including me) will be cultural Catholics until the day we die, filled with the music and architecture and art that were among the many gifts passed to us when young. Those gifts formed the basic template of most New York Catholics, to which we added the gifts of the Jews (above all irony, but also laughter and intellectual toughness) and the Italians (who taught generations of Irish Catholics how to eat, and how to dress, and how to live in an unforgiving world, humanity intact) and the African Americans, who put so much music into all of us, along with the ache of the blues, and a sense of justice that was an American version of so many ancient Irish hopes.

In that sense, every New Yorker is an alloy, and the strength of the alloy is now being passed on to the new immigrants, many of them Catholics, too. They will discover that every New Yorker is a little bit Irish Catholic, a little bit Jewish, a little bit Italian, a little bit African American. The new alloy will also be a little bit Asian and a little bit Latin American. If they could see the city now, my parents, in their different ways, would cheer, and sing, too.

MARY ELIZABETH BROWN

A SEPARATE FEAST

THE ITALIAN INFLUENCE ON CATHOLIC NEW YORK

1

Leo XIII, *Quam Aerumnosa* (December 10, 1887), copy available at "Papal Encyclicals Online," http://www.papalencyclicals.net/ Leo13/l13imi.htm (August 11, 2007).

2

For historical figures, see United States Department of Homeland Security, *Yearbook of Immigration Statistics: 2005* (Washington, D.C.: U.S. Department of Homeland Security, Office of Immigration Statistics, 2006), Table 2, 6–11. For 2006 figure, see U.S. Department of Homeland Security, Office of Immigration Statistics, "Table 2: Persons Obtaining Legal Permanent Status by Region and Selected Country of Last Residence: fiscal years 1820-2006," http://www.dhs.gov/ixmgtn/ statistics/publications/LPR06.shtm (August 4, 2007).

Why highlight Italian immigrants in the history of Catholics in New York City? Immigration statistics suggest that their numbers made the Italians a group to be reckoned with. The fact that they were *Italian* immigrants suggests that they added to archdiocesan diversity. The Italians were also unique because they were, as Pope Leo XIII wrote, "men sprung from the same race as ourselves."[1] The Vatican drew its understanding of migration largely from the Italian example. In New York, archdiocesan experience with Italian immigrants set precedents for ministry to subsequent immigrants. In Italy, experience with Italian migration to New York played a role in the development of organizations for the pastoral care of all migrants.

Two statistics are important for Italian migration. One is the number that entered the United States. In the first decade that the federal government kept such statistics, 1820–1829, 430 persons entered from what is now Italy. Later in the 19th century, the deteriorating Italian economy, coupled with transportation improvements and economic opportunity elsewhere, stimulated immigration, especially after Italian unification in 1870. Italian immigration to the United States rose from 46,296 between 1870 and 1879 to 267,660 in the 1880s, then to 1.9 million in the 1890s, an astonishing increase. War and restrictive immigration policies reduced migration flows from 1920 to 1940. Migration spiked in the 1950s and 1960s, then declined, the most recent annual figure being 3,406 in 2006.[2]

During the ages of sail and steam, most Italians entered the United States through New York harbor, which meant that the Archdiocese of New York bore responsibility for charitable assistance and pastoral care.

The other significant number is that of Italians settling in New York. The 1850 New York State census found 1,039 Italian-born people living in New York City, which at that time meant Manhattan. Between 1870 and 1880, the city grew no larger, but its Italian population went from 3,019 to 13, 411. In 1900, the first year that the federal census included all five boroughs, New York City claimed 145,433 Italian-born residents, with the city's Italian population peaking at 440,250 in 1930.[3]

Two factors complicate these figures. First, people born in the United States might still identify with their Italian roots. The 2000 census, for example, asked about ethnic identity rather than birthplace and found 692,732 people of Italian ancestry residing in New York City.[4] Second, the boundaries of the city and the Archdiocese of New York do not overlap. The 2000 census found 182,226 Italians in Westchester County; 64,450 in Orange; 60,645 in Dutchess; 48,802 in Rockland; 33,629 in Ulster; and 30,441 in Putnam.[5] These people count toward archdiocesan population, but obviously not the city's. The city's Italian population includes those people living in Brooklyn and Queens, but they are part of the Brooklyn Diocese, not the Archdiocese of New York.

Like most immigrant Catholics, Italians brought along distinctive religious customs. They added several feast days to the archdiocesan calendar, including the Feast of St. Joseph's Table (March 19), the Feast of St. Anthony of Padua (June 13), the Feast of Our Lady of Mount Carmel (July 16), and the Feast of San Gennaro (September 19). Italians also added to archdiocesan architectural diversity: St. Anthony of Padua church on Sullivan Street in Manhattan, for example, deliberately used Romanesque instead of the usual Gothic architecture. Our Lady of Pompeii in Greenwich Village and Our Lady of Mount Carmel in White Plains each have a *campanile*, or bell tower, visible as one walks up the street or arrives by train.[6] One Italian creation, the Grotto at Our Lady of Mount Carmel in Rosebank on Staten Island, is on both the state and federal lists of historic sites.

Within the churches themselves, Italians added to the diversity of saints' statues. Christmas crèches are identified with St. Frances of Assisi; and while the custom of setting them up in churches seems to have come to New York with earlier Catholics, New Yorkers saw home crèches as distinctively Italian.[8]

Unlike other immigrant Catholics, the Italians were labeled a "problem" as early as the 1880s. Journalists' observations influenced the first historians of the subject. In 1946, in the first published history of Italian-American Catholicism, historian (and, at the time,

3
Carol Groneman and David M. Reimers, "Population," *Encyclopedia of New York City* (New Haven and New York: Yale University Press and the New-York Historical Society, 1995), 184–185.

4
New York City Department of City Planning, Population Division, "New York City 2000: Results from the 2000 Census, Socioeconomic Characteristics," http://www.nyc.gov/html/dcp/pdf/census/sociopp.pdf (August 4, 2007).

5
National Italian American Foundation (NIAF), "Italian American Populations in Select U.S. Counties," http://www.niaf.org/research/2000_census_1.asp (August 4, 2007). The report did not include Sullivan County, which is part of the Archdiocese of New York. The 2000 census found 73,966 people in Sullivan County, fewer than the Italian population alone of some other counties in the archdiocese. See for Sullivan County population (August 4, 2007). The U.S. Census Bureau's Fact Sheet for Sullivan County gives the figure of 6,142 foreign-born people in the entire county in 2005. See http://factfinder.census.gov (August 4, 2007).

6
St. Anthony of Padua Church, New York City (Hackensack, N.J.: Custombook, 1967), not paginated.

7
National Parks Service, "National Register of Historic Places," Richmond County, New York, page, http://www.nr.nps.gov/iwisapi/explorer (August 13, 2007).

8
"The First Presepion Built by St. Francis," *The New York Times* (December 22, 1912), available through ProQuest (September 10, 2007).

TOP

William F. Farney, [Mulberry Street, "Little Italy," New York], undated

BOTTOM RIGHT

Byron Co., ["Little Italy," New York], 1898

BOTTOM LEFT

A Group of Italians [immigrants], printed in *Harper's Weekly*, October 24, 1891

TOP
J. Ponti, [Celebration of Our Lady of Mount Carmel, East Harlem], 1943
The devotion to *la Madonna del Carmine* in East Harlem began in 1881; the popular *festa* on 115th Street, seen here, continues with support of Haitian pilgrims.

BOTTOM
Vincent La Gambina (1909–1994), *Mott Street*, 1954, oil on canvas
After World War II, celebration of Italian heritage replaced the devotional focus of *feste* like the annual San Gennaro festival in Manhattan.

9

United States Catholic Historical Society *Records and Studies* xxxv (1946), 46-72.

10

Rudolph J. Vecoli, "Prelates and Peasants: Italian Immigrants and the Catholic Church," *Journal of Social History* 11:3 (1969), 217–268.

11

Silvano M. Tomasi, *Piety and Power: The Role of Italian Parishes in the New York Metropolitan Area* (New York: Center for Migration Studies, 1975).

12

Stephen Michael Di Giovanni, "Michael Augustine Corrigan and the Italian Immigrants: The Relationship Between the Church and the Italians in the Archdiocese of New York, 1885–1902" (Ph.D., Gregorian Pontifical University, 1983.) Di Giovanni's dissertation became the basis for his book, *Michael Augustine Corrigan and the Italian Immigrants* (Huntington, Ind.: Our Sunday Visitor, 1994).

13

Robert Anthony Orsi, "The Madonna of 115th Street: Faith and Community in Italian Harlem, 1880–1950" (Ph.D., Yale University, 1982). This became the basis of his book of the same name, published by Yale in 1985.

14

Edward C. Stibili, *"What Can Be Done To Help Them?" The Italian Saint Raphael Society, 1887–1923* (New York: Center for Migration Studies, 2003).

15

Peter R. D'Agostino, *Rome in America: Transnational Catholic Ideology from the Risorgimento to Fascism* (Chapel Hill: The University of North Carolina Press, 2004).

16

Giovanni Batista Scalabrini, *L'Emigrazione Italiana in America* (Piacenza: Tip. dell'Amico del Popolo, 1887). The pamphlet is reprinted in the original Italian in the published collection of Scalabrini's writing, *Scritti* I (Rome: Centro Studi Emigrazione, 1980), 18–71, and in English in Silvano M. Tomasi, c.s., *For the Love of Immigrants: Migration Writings and Letters of Bishop John Baptist Scalabrin (1839–1901)* (New York: Center for Migration Studies, 2000), 1–31.

New York priest) Henry Browne summarized the complaints of 19th-century pastors about Italian immigrants. They did not attend Mass, receive the sacraments, educate their offspring in the faith, contribute to the support of their parishes, enter the priesthood or religious orders in significant numbers, or realize that they should have been doing all these things.[9] A generation later, historian Rudolph J. Vecoli argued that the problem lay with Catholicism itself: Its prelates neglected the Italian peasantry, stimulating both folk and radical anticlericalism, and the anti-Italian prejudices of its American priests and laity gave Italians no reason to feel part of the community of faith.[10] Other scholars have studied how various parties attempted to solve this problem. Sociologist Silvano M. Tomasi acknowledged the role of Italian immigrants who fought for and got their own parishes where they could assimilate at their own pace, usually under the care of Italian migrant clergy.[11] Historian Stephen Michael Di Giovanni credited New York's archbishop Michael Augustine Corrigan, who served from 1885 to 1900, for recruiting religious orders that supplied Italian-speaking clergy and supporting the clergy as they ministered to Italian immigrants, first in "annex congregations" meeting in basement chapels of established parishes and then in parishes of their own.[12]

Robert A. Orsi advanced Italian-American Catholic scholarship in his study of the feast of Our Lady of Mount Carmel in East Harlem; he switched the focus from what the Italians did not do to what they did.[13] Most recently, while working independently, historians Edward C. Stibili and Peter R. D'Agostino each have put Italian immigration into a transnational context. Stibili's study of the St. Raphael Society for the Protection of Italian Immigrants shows one practical way that Italian Catholics in Italy expressed solidarity with compatriots and coreligionists *nel mondo*, a phrase Italians use for Italians outside Italy.[14] The late Professor D'Agostino argued that the Vatican judged every development, including Italian migration, in the light of its commitment to a Christian civilization that transcended the recent creation of nation-states.[15] Consideration of the Italians in New York, then, has to take into account the different viewpoints of the place the Italians came from and the place to which they came.

The Vatican was getting some of its information from Giovanni Battista Scalabrini, bishop of Piacenza, a diocese in Emilia-Romagna. In 1887, Scalabrini published the first of several pamphlets on Italian migration to the Americas.[16] In it, he recounted passing through the Milan railway station and being struck by the waiting room full of impoverished working men and women, waiting for trains that would take them to port cities, where they would sail to other places in search of work. While Scalabrini accepted migration as a solution to the problem of poverty in Italy, he condemned the fact that the poor remained vulnerable both to starvation wages and the price-gouging travel industry.[17] He asked the Italian government to protect migrants as laborers and consumers, and the Church to send clergy to accompany the migrants in transit and in their new homes. Scalabrini had no role in decid-

SAN ROCCO

PROTETTORE DI SAVOIA LUCANIA

LA CUI FESTA SI CELEBRA AL No. 293 MOTT ST.,
IL 15 E 16 AGOSTO DI OGNI ANNO, PER CURA DELLA
SOCIETA' SAN ROCCO DI MUTUO SOCCORSO
TRA I CITTADINI DI SAVOIA LUCANIA IN NEW YORK

EXCELLO TYPOGRAPHICAL CO., INC., 65 FOURTH AVE., NEW YORK

Broadside, undated, hand-colored woodcut on paper

This broadside announces the annual celebration of the feast of "Saint Rocco Protector of Savoia Lucania" at 293 Mott Street, on the 15th and 16th of August by the St. Rocco Mutual Aid Society and the citizens of Savoia Luciana in New York.

TOP

[Celebrating the Feast of San Rocco, in Bandit's Roost, Mulberry Bend], 1895

Immigrant Italian Catholics retained traditional devotions, such as the *festa* honoring the hometown or provincial patron saint.

ing the places to which the migrants went. What he hoped for was that the anticlerical Italian government would reconcile itself to the Church, and the two institutions would cooperate in perpetuating Christian civilization among the migrants and spreading it in the places where the migrants settled.

Practicing what he preached, Scalabrini organized a congregation of male religious to be missionaries, as he called them, to Italian Catholics abroad. Initially, his plans called for the laity to organize committees to assist travelers at Italian and American ports, and for the clergy to pick central locations where they would live communally and from which they would visit scattered Italian settlements. However, Pope Leo XIII insisted on more clerical leadership, and so instead of port committees, individual clergy were stationed at ports.[18] The most pertinent modification of Scalabrini's plan, though, took place after the first missionaries arrived in the United States.

Archbishop Corrigan was already communicating with Scalabrini regarding his plans. On January 7, 1888, Scalabrini sent Father Marcellino Moroni to New York with a letter of introduction asking Corrigan to place Moroni where he might be most useful for the Italian missions.[19] Corrigan made Moroni an assistant at Transfiguration parish on Mott Street near lower Manhattan's Little Italy. Moroni's experience suggested reasons to modify Scalabrini's plan. First, there were deep divisions between the Italian immigrants and the non-Italian pastors in parishes where the Italians settled. The pastors feared a special Italian ministry would prevent Italians from integrating into their parishes and helping to sustain those parishes spiritually and economically. They also did not want to provide the welcome that would attach the Italians to the parishes in the first place. Second, divisions among Italians, especially northern disdain for southerners, argued against unified Italian parishes. Scalabrini continued to think in terms of an Italian rather than a regional identity, but he gave up the idea of clergy visiting scattered congregations in favor of national parishes. He suggested to Corrigan that the first missionaries in New York live communally and establish a chapel that would gather Italians from surrounding non-Italian parishes and eventually become a parish in its own right, plus staff the nonparochial port ministry.[20]

Three missionaries, led by Felix Morelli, landed in New York on July 22, 1888, and implemented the first stage of the plan, opening Resurrection chapel. By Christmas Eve, they had moved on to the second stage, opening St. Joachim parish on Roosevelt Street (razed in 1956 to make way for Police Plaza and a new approach to the Brooklyn Bridge). In 1891, Morelli expanded to a second parish, Most Precious Blood on Baxter Street in Little Italy, opened Columbus Hospital, then on East 109th Street, and bought land for a seminary. Meanwhile, Pietro Bandini arrived to set up the port ministry, called the St. Raphael Society for the Protection of Italian Immigrants.

17
Scalabrini was not alone. The most thorough monograph on Italian migrant labor is probably still Robert F. Foerster, *The Italian Emigration of Our Times,* Harvard Economic Studies XX (Cambridge, Massachusetts: Harvard University Press, 1924). For Italian immigrants *qua* travelers, see Augusta Molinari, "Emigration Traffic in the Port of Genoa Between the Nineteenth and Twentieth Centuries: Shipping and Problems of Social Hygiene," *Journal of American Ethnic History* XIII:1 (Fall 1993), 102–115.

18
Mario Francesconi, c.s., "Initial Phases of the Scalabrinian Congregation, 1886–1888," trans. M. Bartolozzo (typescript 1983), 36–37.

19
Giovanni Batista Scalabrini to Michael Augustine Corrigan, Piacenza, January 7, 1888, Giovanni Batista Scalabrini, *Scritti* I, 88–89.

20
Scalabrini to Corrigan, Piacenza, February 25, 1888, *Scritti* I, 93–94.

Giovanni Battista Scalabrini, Bishop of Piacenza, undated
Bishop Scalabrini, from Emilia-Romagna, Italy, founded the male religious order Missionaries of St. Charles (known as the Scalabrinians) to minister to Italian immigrants.

Antonio Demo, P.S.S.C., undated
Demo served as pastor of Our Lady of Pompeii from 1899 to 1933.

Larry Racioppo, *Our Lady of Mount Carmel Grotto, Rosebank, Staten Island*, 1999
This privately built grotto is listed on both the New York State and National Registers of Historic Places.

**John Costanza, *Italian Festa*, c. 1960,
oil on masonite**
Feste often included a band, food vendors,
balloons, and game stalls, as well as
an image of the saint being honored,
as at this celebration on 12th Street
between First Avenue and Avenue A,
depicted about 1930.

21
Di Giovanni, "Michael Augustine Corrigan," 310–338.

22
Sullivan, 92–94, 116–117.

23
New York Evening Post (July 19, 1906), clipping in Center for Migration Studies Collection #079, Box 5, Folder 124.

24
Di Giovanni, "Michael Augustine Corrigan," 373.

25
"La Guida del Clero Italiano di New York," *Il Carroccio* II (1915), 76–77.

26
"Agreement between Italica Gens (Italian Auxiliary, Inc.) and NCWC," New York, July 28, 1923, CMS Coll. #023, Box 36, "Italian Auxiliary" folder.

27
Thomas Mulholland to Bruce Mohler, New York, May 31, 1934, ibid. Mohler was director of the NCWC Bureau of Immigration. Mulholland was director of the Bureau's New York Port Office.

28
"Minutes of Meetings with Pastors of Italian Congregations Held in 1902–1903," CMS Coll. #019, Box 1, "Miscellaneous Correspondence Regarding Italians" folder.

29
"Diocesan Bureaux for the Care of Italian, Slav, Ruthenian, and Asian Catholics in America," *Ecclesiastical Review* XLVIII (1913), 221–222.

30
Il Carroccio XIII (1921), 683, and *The New York Times* (May 6, 1921), 13.

Then everything almost collapsed. Precious Blood's debts came due and could be paid only by declaring bankruptcy and reorganizing the mission, with the Franciscans supplying the clergy.[21] Columbus Hospital's debts were paid off when Mother Cabrini purchased the hospital for her order.[22] St. Joachim's debts were less pressing, but Morelli had sown the seeds for future problems through contracts with multiple mutual benefit societies. Italian men organized these societies to sponsor annual feast day celebrations of the patron saint of their hometown or region in Italy, and to provide health or life insurance for members. The contracts called for St. Joachim's to house the saints' statues and to provide religious services in exchange for annual fees. In 1906, the St. Rocco Society divided over whether to renew its contract with St. Joachim's, and unseemly reports of Italians kidnapping statues and going to court against their pastor made it into the English-language press.[23] Meanwhile, the chapel of Our Lady of Pompeii, which Bandini had organized as part of his port ministry, had grown into a parish, but Bandini had finished his short-term commitment to the mission, putting the parish in danger. Pompeii survived due to the financial support of a devout Catholic heiress, Annie Leary.[24]

The lesson Corrigan took away from the situation was the importance of monitoring Italian clergy. He already had a potential supervisor for them. In 1891, Corrigan appointed a priest named Gherardo Ferrante to serve as his Italian secretary. (Corrigan could read, but not write, Italian.) Over time, Ferrante took on the duties of overseeing Italian religious orders and the pastoral care of Italians passing through the port as well as Italians living in parishes.[25] Since that time, port and parish ministry have become separate. In 1921, the new National Catholic Welfare Conference began taking responsibility for issues that crossed diocesan boundaries, such as the care of immigrants. In 1923, Scalabrini's adherents closed the St. Raphael Society, and between then and 1934 Catholic Charities of the Archdiocese of New York collaborated with an Italian-based organization, Italica Gens, in supporting the Italian Auxiliary, which provided care specifically to Italian immigrants.[26] The Italian Auxiliary, and all diocesan-level care for Italians coming through the port of New York, ended with the retirement of the director of the Auxiliary, Monsignor Germano Formica.[27]

The history of the care of Italians in archdiocesan parishes is more convoluted. Corrigan's successor, John Murphy (later Cardinal) Farley, turned Ferrante's one-man job into a bureaucracy. In 1902, Farley began by calling meetings among pastors with Italians in their parishes, but meetings ceased within a year.[28] In 1913, Farley organized the Italian Bureau, which provided greater supervision and also served as a forum for dialogue with clergy involved in Italian migrant care.[29] While an Irish American, Michael Joseph Lavelle, presided over the Italian Bureau, Ferrante was its most active member. Cardinal Farley died in 1918, and Monsignor Ferrante in 1921. Farley's successor, Patrick Joseph (later Cardinal) Hayes, did not replace Ferrante, and the Italian Bureau disappeared from the archdiocesan organizational chart in 1927.[30] By the 1930s, the archdiocese no longer needed close supervision of Italian clergy. Italian Americans were moving into the priesthood; at least three Italian-American alumni of St. Joseph Seminary founded parishes in the 1920s.[31] Also the most successful Italian-born and -trained clergy had assimilated. Antonio Demo, for whom the plaza across from the church of Our Lady of Pompeii in Greenwich Village is named, came to resemble the image of the Irish-American pastor, a community leader and the builder of a church, rectory, and parochial school.[32]

Bishop Scalabrini's experience with New York and other mission stations reinforced what he already believed. The Catholic Church was built for stability, with the Christian world divided into dioceses, the dioceses divided into parishes, and people assigned to parishes on a geographical basis. Territorial parishes marginalized the transient population that uneven economic development created. In 1905, Scalabrini wrote to the Vatican about extending the model he had developed for the Italians to other ethnic Catholics, providing linguistic and cultural continuity for all uprooted people.[33] Scalabrini died later that year. Within ten years, World War I suppressed the migration that had so concerned him, but Scalabrini's message was not forgotten. The displacement that came after the two world wars, when added to the continuing uneven economic development, made migration more important than ever, and stimulated the creation of the Pontifical Commission on Migrants and Itinerant People.

This account of the development of Italian pastoral care cannot conclude without considering one final issue. Who was to pay for the pastoral care of recent arrivals? While Corrigan was personally generous to the Italian ministry, he expected parishes to be self-supporting. Charities such as the St. Raphael Society depended on their own donors. Financial need created a situation whereby the Italians required services but could not pay for them. The archdiocesan approach to parish economics was an important factor in reducing the influence of experimental efforts such as the St. Raphael Society and in leading the Italians to create their own national parishes. Since they controlled the purse strings of these parishes, they had some say over which saints to honor and how to honor them.

Scalabrini saw that the American system of financing religious practice was a kind of capitalism: People who could pay got service, and people who could not did not always get exactly what they needed. His search for words to express the issue led him to another American archbishop, who enunciated an ambitious program of which pastoral care of Italian immigrants was only one element. In his 1887 pamphlet on Italian migration, Scalabrini quoted approvingly Cardinal James Gibbons, archbishop of Baltimore: "[T]he great questions of the future are not those of war, of commerce or finance, but the social questions, the questions which concern the improvement of the conditions of the great masses of the people, and especially of the working people, it is evidently of supreme importance that the Church should always be found on the side of humanity, of justice toward the multitudes that compose the body of the human family."[34]

31
Victor Bassi founded Our Lady of Grace in the Bronx; Bonaventure Filetti founded both St. Theresa of the Infant Jesus and St. Benedicta on Staten Island; Emil E. Molinelli founded St. Michael and St. Clement on Staten Island.
32
The bulk of CMS Coll. #037 consists of Demo's papers regarding the administration of Our Lady of Pompeii.
33
Bishop Scalabrini's Plan for the Pastoral Care of Migrants of All Nationalities (New York: Center for Migration Studies, undated). This pamphlet combines in one place and in English translation various pieces of correspondence between Scalabrini and officials in the Vatican curia.
34
Scalabrini, *L'Emigrazione Italiana in America, Scritti* I, 71. The translation used is from the Catholic University of America, American Catholic History Classroom, Document #18, http://libraries.cua.edu/achrcua/Knights/kol_doc18.html (August 15, 2007). The translation in Tomasi, *For the Love of Migrants*, 31, used the word "economy" for "finance," rendering the passage more difficult to understand.

TOP

Carrying the image of Saint Rocco in procession along Roosevelt Street outside St. Joachim's church, August 16, 1933

BOTTOM LEFT

Marjory Collins, [Italian family on the steps of a Catholic church in the Bronx], 1943
As Italians moved out of lower Manhattan, new parishes opened in Queens, the Bronx, and Brooklyn.

BOTTOM RIGHT

Procession outside the Church of Our Lady of Carmel, Williamsburg, Brooklyn, 1959
Immigrants from Nola, Italy, introduced the feast of St. Paulinus, with its *giglio* [lily] tower and boat, to Williamsburg in 1903.

39

PATRICK J. McNAMARA

A PEOPLE SET APART

THE CHURCH GROWS IN BROOKLYN...AND QUEENS

1
"Some Ancient History: Catholicity in Brooklyn Sixty Years Ago," *Brooklyn Eagle,* January 17, 1892, 13.

2
"A Sketch of Some of the Catholic Churches in Queens and Suffolk Counties," *Brooklyn Eagle,* January 16, 1879, 1.

3
"Concerning the Historical Records of the Diocese—Other Notes," unidentified newsclipping (1893?), in BK 110 SS Peter & Paul file, Parish Files, Msgr. John K. Sharp Collection, Archives of the Diocese of Brooklyn (hereafter ADB). See also John T. Ridge, "When Williamsburg and Greenpoint Were Irish," *New York Irish History* 10 (1996): 14–20.

4
Farewell Address of Rev. Sylvester Malone, to His Congregation, in Sts. Peter and Paul's Church, Brooklyn, E.D., N.Y., Sunday Morning, May 29, 1881, Preceding His Departure for a Prolonged Visit to Europe (Brooklyn, 1881), 3, in BK 110 SS Peter & Paul file, Parish Files, Sharp Collection, ADB.

In 1836, the city of Brooklyn was still obscure enough for the U.S. *Catholic Almanac* to list it as "Brookland" without any local repercussions. A reporter for the *Brooklyn Eagle* who noted the error some 60 years later suggested that there probably weren't enough Catholics around at the time to notice. He wasn't far off the mark.[1] Brooklyn in 1836 had two Catholic churches. Queens, Nassau, and Suffolk counties had none, so priests rode a circuit across Long Island, celebrating Mass in places where, the *Eagle* noted, "there was no railroad or talk of one."[2]

In 1830, the village of Williamsburg had ten Catholic families who took the Manhattan ferry to church.[3] Eight years later, a priest from Manhattan celebrated Williamsburg's first Mass in a stable. In October 1841, Father Johann Raffeiner, a Napoleonic Wars veteran, founded Most Holy Trinity parish on Montrose Avenue, for the growing German population. When newly ordained Sylvester Malone came to Saints Peter and Paul parish in 1844, he noted that the Irish were the minority among Williamsburg Catholics. "We could not see at the time," he wrote later, "what the dreadful famine in Ireland in '47 and '48 would do in filling up the unoccupied spaces of the two great cities, New York and Brooklyn."[4]

By 1853, one third of all Kings County residents spoke with Irish brogues or German accents.[5] That year, ten new American dioceses were founded to meet the needs of a growing population. On July 29, the Diocese of Brooklyn was established, as Long Island was separated from the New York Archdiocese. New York's vicar general, Father John Loughlin, was named bishop. At 36, he was one of the youngest members of the hierarchy.[6] During

Loughlin's 38-year tenure, an impressive network of churches, schools, hospitals, and orphanages arose from Red Hook to the Hamptons, as the Catholic population of Long Island grew from 15,000 to 280,000.

When Sylvester Malone celebrated his silver jubilee at Saints Peter and Paul in 1869, an impressive Gothic church was in place, a dozen women religious ran a parochial school of 1,500, and the parish was a center of community life. With some justification could he boast:

> When we came together in this parish a quarter of a century ago, we were not worth a cent financially. We had no lands, no edifices; but God has prospered us, and we have now a flourishing parish, and surrounding us are eleven other churches.[7]

This phenomenon was not confined to Williamsburg. In Bedford-Stuyvesant, Vincentian priests founded St. Mary Queen of the Isle parish in July 1868. Within a generation, a cathedral-like edifice (larger than the actual diocesan cathedral) replaced the original frame building. By then, the parish grounds housed a parochial school, high school, college, and seminary.[8] Theoretically, a young man could receive all his sacraments, attend school from first grade through college, study for the priesthood, and be ordained on the same block. The Vincentians had also renamed the parish St. John the Baptist in honor of the bishop, John Loughlin. Notorious for his dislike of religious orders, Loughlin seems to have made an exception for them.[9]

None of this growth came without a struggle. One study of antebellum Brooklyn estimates that Williamsburg alone had 60 nativist organizations. On April 5, 1844, the *Brooklyn Eagle* described a riot that had broken out the night before on Court Street in downtown Brooklyn between the "Native Americans"[10] and groups of Catholic immigrants, which ended with the arrival of the militia. Such incidents were repeated all too often during the next decade.[11]

The summer of 1854 witnessed an outburst known as the Angel Gabriel Riot, on the corner of Smith Street and Atlantic Avenue. The riot was the work of John S. Orr, a nativist who called himself "the Angel Gabriel" and addressed Brooklyn crowds while dressed in white robes and carrying a trumpet. The *Eagle* described Orr's approach:

> Orr started off by pitching into the Pope, as usual, applying all sorts of abuse to him, and characterizing him as a tyrant who would never be satisfied until he had set his foot on the necks of all free born American citizens. After going on in this strain for some time he blew a blast on his horn and invited those who sympathized with him in singing doggerel verses of his own make, the refrain of which was "We'll chain the Pope to the other side of the Jordan."…[He then] proceeded to make the sweeping assertion that all the Sons

5
John K. Sharp, *History of the Diocese of Brooklyn, 1853–1953: The Catholic Church on Long Island*. 2 vols. (New York: Fordham University Press, 1954), 2:166.

6
Joseph W. Coen, Patrick J. McNamara, and Peter I. Vaccari, *Diocese of Immigrants: The Brooklyn Catholic Experience, 1853–2003* (Strasbourg: Éditions du Signe, 2004), 27. See also Francis B. Donnelly, "Erection of the Diocese of Brooklyn: A Providential Afterthought," *U.S. Catholic Historian* 1, no. 4 (fall 1981): 106–32.

7
"St. Peter and St. Paul's Church," unidentified newsclipping, August 21, 1869, in BK 110 SS Peter & Paul file, Parish Files, John K. Sharp Collection, ADB.

8
St. John's College opened in 1870 on the parish grounds. In 1933, it achieved university status, and in 1954 the main campus moved to Queens, where it remains today.

9
In 1889, a *Brooklyn Eagle* reporter commented: "The Bishop has an aversion for two classes of people—Jesuits and reporters"; see "Bishop Loughlin's Ways," *Brooklyn Eagle*, December 4, 1889, 4. Loughlin felt that the Jesuits were stealing vocations from the diocese; see Thomas J. Campbell, S.J., to Thomas F. Meehan, September 14, 1891, in Thomas F. Meehan Papers, folder 1, box 1, Special Collections Division, Lauinger Library, Georgetown Univeristy, Washington, D.C.

10
The term *Native American* had a far different meaning in 19th-century America than it does now, as it often referred to native-born white Anglo-Saxon Protestants. For further background, see Richard J. Purcell and John F. Poole, "Political Nativism in Brooklyn," *Journal of the American-Irish Historical Society* 31 (1931): 48.

11
Brooklyn Eagle, April 5, 1844, 2. The *Eagle* blamed the Nativists for the unrest. Throughout the 19th century, the paper's coverage of Catholicism was often favorable and fair, without being uncritical.

PAGE 40

St. James Cathedral-Basilica, 1948
St. James is one of three Catholic cathedrals within the borough of Brooklyn.

TOP LEFT

Church of Saints Peter and Paul, Williamsburg, Brooklyn, c. 1880
Rev. Sylvester Malone chose architect Patrick J. Keely to design the gothic building at South 3rd and Wythe streets. Bishop John Hughes laid the cornerstone in 1847.

TOP RIGHT

St. John the Baptist church, 1868
The parish of St. John the Baptist opened at Willoughby and Lewis streets in Bedford-Stuyvesant, Brooklyn, in 1868 staffed by the Vincentian order.

RIGHT, MIDDLE

St. John the Baptist parish with church, grammar school, high school, college, and seminary, 1900
By 1900, St. John's College (founded in 1870, now St. John's University), adjacent to the parish, filled the corner of Willoughby and Lewis streets.

BOTTOM LEFT

Father Sylvester Malone, pastor of Saints Peter and Paul in Williamsburg, 1854
Father Malone (1821–1899) served as the church's pastor from 1844 to 1899. For most of the 19th century, many Catholic priests dressed like their Protestant counterparts, in suits and ties, as seen here.

BOTTOM RIGHT

Portrait of Father John Loughlin, 1860s
Father Loughlin (1817–1891) served as Brooklyn's first bishop from 1853 to 1891. A native of Ireland, he presided over an ever-growing immigrant diocese.

TOP
Procession from St. Michael's, a German national parish, Brooklyn, 1905

BOTTOM LEFT
Sunday School Class, St. Peter Claver, 1920s
Father Bernard J. Quinn (top left), founded Brooklyn's first African-American parish, St. Peter Claver, in Bedford-Stuyvesant in 1920.

BOTTOM RIGHT
La Sociedad del Santo Nombre members, c. 1940
Puerto Ricans from Brooklyn's Our Lady of Pilar church formed a Spanish-language *Sociedad del Santo Nombre* [Holy Name Society] by 1935.

12
"A Bigot With a Bugle: The Angel Gabriel Riots of Many Years Ago," *Brooklyn Eagle*, November 10, 1889, 10. See also Sharp, *History of the Diocese of Brooklyn*, 1:273–75. At Most Holy Trinity, Father Raffeiner stationed armed parishioners around the church. The parish history comments: "In these stirring times the martial spirit of the old soldier-pastor of Holy Trinity came back to inspire his devoted flock to take measures to ensure the safety of their lives and property"; *The Most Holy Trinity Parish in the Diocese of Brooklyn, N.Y., 1841–1916: Three Quarters of a Century of Progress, Spiritual and Temporal* (Brooklyn, 1916), 10.

13
For the quotations, see Sharp, *History of the Diocese of Brooklyn*, 1:227, 2:38–39.

14
Betty Smith, *A Tree Grows in Brooklyn* (New York: Harper and Brothers, 1943), 390.

15
Shortly after McDonnell's appointment was announced, the *Eagle* noted that a group of Brooklyn priests made "a vigorous demand for Home Rule"; "Charles E. McDonnell Succeeds John Loughlin," *Brooklyn Eagle*, March 11, 1892, 6.

16
For further background, see Sharp, *History of the Diocese of Brooklyn*, 2:43–50.

17
My survey of *Sadlier's Catholic Directory* for 1892 showed that 131 of Brooklyn's 184 diocesan priests had identifiably Irish names—approximately 71 percent of the total population; *Sadlier's Catholic Directory, Almanac and Ordo for the Year of Our Lord 1892* (New York: D. & J. Sadlier, 1892), 198–204. For the Irish-born statistics, see Sharp, *History of the Diocese of Brooklyn*, 2:321.

of St. Patrick were slaves of the Pope and serpents in disguise who should be driven out of the country without delay.[12]

As the Civil War approached, nativism lost its appeal (albeit temporarily), and Catholics found greater acceptance in the "City of Churches." In October 1872, the *Catholic Review* observed: "To the non-Catholic inhabitants...a 'Romish Church' is no longer a thing of wonderment, a Romish priest is no longer a stranger." In December 1877, the *Boston Christian Register* commented,

> [Brooklyn] might well be called a Catholic city. The Roman Church here has more houses of worship than any other.... Most of these Brooklyn Churches are large and costly, and many of them are magnificent in architecture and decorations.[13]

By the end of the 19th century, well before the phrase "megachurch" was coined, many Brooklyn parishes fit that description. In her 1943 novel, *A Tree Grows in Brooklyn*, Betty Smith (born Elizabeth Wehner in Williamsburg in 1896) offers an almost exact description of her childhood parish, Most Holy Trinity:

> Francie thought it was the most beautiful church in Brooklyn. It was made of old gray stone and had twin spires that rose cleanly into the sky, high above the tallest tenements. Inside, the high vaulted ceilings, narrow deepset stained-glass windows and elaborately carved altars made it a miniature cathedral.[14]

Her church, known as Brooklyn's "German Cathedral," encompassed a rectory, parochial school, high school, convent, and orphanage. From 1869 to 1872, it published a daily newspaper (in German).

In 1892, to the chagrin of many Brooklyn priests, another Manhattanite was named bishop of Brooklyn.[15] At the age of 37, Charles E. McDonnell was America's youngest bishop. A protégé of Cardinal John McCloskey, he shared the cardinal's elegance, wit, and dislike for publicity. During World War I, for example, he agreed to participate in a fund drive, but only on the condition that he not be required to deliver speeches.[16]

McDonnell was a capable administrator. In short order, he appointed a superintendent of schools and a director of Catholic Charities. In 1893, Brooklyn's first monsignor was named, Michael May, and in 1909 the first auxiliary bishop, George Mundelein. Both were Germans, a bit of a surprise in a diocese where seven out of ten priests had Irish ancestry (with Irish-born clergy composing more than one third of the total number of priests). Mundelein was named archbishop of Chicago in 1915, and nine years later became a cardinal. (He is the only Brooklyn priest to have a town named after him: Mundelein, Illinois.)[17]

Bishop Molloy enters Brooklyn's Ebbets Field at
a Holy Name Society rally, c. 1940

As the diocese's population approached one million, immigration was its biggest challenge. Journalist Thomas F. Meehan, who spent seven decades chronicling Brooklyn Catholic life, wrote in 1911 that Catholicism on Long Island resembled

> [a] perpetual Pentecost, for the Gospel is preached to the faithful in twelve languages. Polish, French, Italian, German, Slav, Syrian, Greek, Hungarian, Lithuanian, Scandinavian, Bohemian, as well as English-speaking Catholics...have special ministrations for their respective nationalities.[18]

In McDonnell's 29 years as bishop, 35 parishes were founded for Italians, Poles, and Lithuanians, as were three Eastern Rite parishes.[19]

The new parishes had humble beginnings. By the turn of the century, Lithuanians living near the Navy Yard were worshiping in the basement of St. Ann's, the Irish parish. Soon the basement was no longer adequate, and in 1909 they started their own church, St. George. In Ozone Park, Italian Catholics gathered for Mass at the home of Carmine Napolitano on Shoe Leather Street. When his living room became too small, they purchased property for Nativity of the Blessed Virgin Mary, which went up in 1906. Around 1903, Maronites (Arabic-speaking Catholics) began gathering in a house on Cobble Hill that seven years later was dedicated as a church. Today, Our Lady of Lebanon Cathedral, Brooklyn Heights, is one of the borough's three Catholic cathedrals, along with St. James Cathedral-Basilica and St. Ann's Armenian Cathedral in Williamsburg.[20]

During the war years, a systematic outreach to African Americans and Hispanics evolved. In 1916, Spanish priests founded Our Lady of Pilar for Brooklyn's growing Puerto Rican community, and seminarians went to Spain for language immersion. In 1915, Brooklyn's African-American Catholics organized the Colored Catholic Club and petitioned McDonnell for a parish. In 1920, Father Bernard J. Quinn, who was long interested in ministering to black Catholics, established St. Peter Claver in Bedford-Stuyvesant. In 1932, he helped found another African-American parish in Queens, St. Benedict the Moor.

During World War I, Quinn developed a strong devotion to Thérèse of Lisieux, whose autobiography he read while stationed in France as an army chaplain. Shortly before her canonization in 1925, he started a shrine in her honor at St. Peter Claver, one of the first in New York. Its novenas attracted Catholics from the entire metropolitan area. White Catholics from throughout the city traveled to the "Negro Church," whose neighboring parish, Nativity of Our Blessed Lord, excluded blacks. By 1930, the *Brooklyn Eagle* estimated that more than two million people had visited the shrine.[21]

18
Thomas F. Meehan, "Brooklyn, Diocese of," *The Catholic Encyclopedia: An International Work of Reference on the Constitution, Doctrine, Discipline, and History of the Catholic Church.* 15 vols. and index (New York: Encyclopedia Press, 1913), 2:798. A later diocesan historian commented similarly that "the tongues of many nations were soon likened to the first Pentecost"; Sharp, *History of the Diocese of Brooklyn*, 2:78.

19
The older immigrant groups did not always react positively to these changes. In 1910, Paul Boyton from Coney Island wrote a letter to the bishop, complaining that "a grave injustice has been done to the non-Italian members of the Church of Our Lady of Solace, by turning it over to an Italian priest. The Americans resent it as an insult"; Paul Boyton to Charles E. McDonnell, May 29, 1910, in "Italian Immigration, 1888–1919, c. 248-E-1," Canon Law Subject Files, ADB. By "Americans" the writer presumably meant "Irish."

20
On St. George, see Casimir E. Paulonis to John K. Sharp, September 9, 1944, in St. George file, box 1, John K. Sharp Collection, ADB. For Nativity, see "Parish History Questionnaire," in Nativity of the BVM file, Chancery Parish Files, Box 7, ADB. (The name "Shoe Leather Street" has not been in use since Queens streets were numbered.) On the genesis of Our Lady of Lebanon, see Sharp, *History of the Diocese of Brooklyn*, 2:84.

21
Paul W. Jervis, *Quintessential Priest: The Life of Father Bernard J. Quinn* (Strasbourg: Éditions du Signe, 2005), 124–37. Catholics from outside the parish helped raise money for the shrine. Irish-American historian John T. Ridge recalls that his mother belonged to one such group, the League of White Women. On the tension between Quinn and his neighboring parish, see John T. McGreevey, *Parish Boundaries: The Catholic Encounter with Race in the Twentieth Century Urban North* (Chicago: University of Chicago Press, 1996), 55–56.

22

Elliott Willensky, *When Brooklyn Was the World, 1920–1957* (New York: Harmony Books, 1986), 11, 13.

23

Sharp, *History of the Diocese of Brooklyn,* 2:165, 166. See also McGreevey, *Parish Boundaries,* 15.

24

"Archbishop Thomas Edmund Molloy," 2. See also John K. Sharp, *An Old Priest Remembers, 1892–1978* (Hicksville, N.Y.: Extension Press, 1978).

25

Elliot Willensky comments: "Big, klutzy Brooklyn always seemed to be playing second fiddle to svelte Manhattan"; Willensky, *When Brooklyn Was the World,* 20.

26

"In a Clergyman's Study: The Home of Bishop Loughlin, of Brooklyn," *Brooklyn Eagle,* October 7, 1888, 10.

27

"Bishop McDonnell, Our Second Ordinary," *One Hundredth Anniversary, Roman Catholic Diocese of Brooklyn, 1853–1953* (Brooklyn: The Tablet, 1953), 15.

28

"Archbishop Thomas Edmund Molloy: Man of Action and Contemplation" (unpublished ms.), 2, in Bishop's Files, Box 5023, *Tablet* Collection, ADB.

29

James A. Rooney, "Catholicity in Queens," *Progress of the Catholic Church on Long Island: Queens County Section (Supplement to The Tablet),* July 22, 1916, 7. On the borough's expansion, see Jon A. Peterson and Vincent Seyfried, "Queens," in Kenneth T. Jackson, ed., *The Encyclopedia of New York City* (New Haven, Conn.: Yale University Press, 1995), 969.

In February 1922, a native son, 36-year-old Thomas E. Molloy, succeeded McDonnell. His 34-year episcopate coincided with a period that Brooklyn historian Elliott Willensky calls Brooklyn's "golden age." [22] By 1930, Catholicism was Kings County's largest religious denomination, claiming 35 percent of the population. At the time of the 1953 centennial, the diocesan population was nearly 1.4 million, a number surpassed only in the archdioceses of Boston and Chicago. [23] Rumors abounded that Brooklyn would soon be raised to archdiocesan status. Although this never happened, Molloy was named an honorary archbishop in 1951.

A dignified, imposing figure, Molloy was remembered by contemporaries as a "master administrator," "an orator without peer," and a "brilliant personality." New York's Cardinal Patrick Hayes once said that there was no bishop quite like Molloy. With Molloy, it was said, the "attitude that one would go to Brooklyn only to be buried was soon changed." Like his predecessor, he avoided all publicity. In 1936, he bought one of the Pratt mansions in Clinton Hill, where he lived by himself for the next 20 years. [24]

Brooklyn Catholics remained in the shadow of the archdiocese. (Many continue to be unaware that New York is the only American city to encompass two dioceses.) [25] Brooklyn Catholics could be touchy over any statement by the cardinal that made the front page, but their bishops preferred it that way. They avoided the spotlight and went about their work. In 1888, a *Brooklyn Eagle* reporter wrote of Bishop Loughlin:

> To obtain any information from the reverend gentleman, no matter how trivial may be the subject upon which knowledge is desired, is as hopeless a task as a newspaper man has to contend with in the course of his varied experiences. [26]

McDonnell, it was said, "shunned publicity as much as he could, and yielded not to the glamour of the public forum." [27] Cardinal Spellman's views on public issues were well known, but Molloy "never took a public stand, stayed away from controversy, and ran his diocese." [28]

At the turn of the 20th century, before subway lines, the Brooklyn-Queens Expressway, and the Triborough Bridge came along, much of Queens was undeveloped farmland. But things were changing by World War I. In 1916, *The Tablet* optimistically described the borough as a "future Catholic stronghold." During the 1920s, as Queens's population passed the one million mark, houses and churches went up at unprecedented rates. More parishes were founded there during the 1920s than during the entire 19th century.

Still, *The Tablet* admitted, Queens could sometimes be "a soil none too congenial." [29] In 1896, the property for Saints Joachim and Anne church in Queens Village had to be purchased

TOP LEFT

Advertisment from *The Tablet*, **undated**
The Tablet, the Brooklyn diocesan news-
paper, promoted parish-wide Holy Name
Society membership.

TOP RIGHT

The Tablet, **July 21, 1923**
Anti-Catholicism fostered by the Ku Klux
Klan erupted in Queens and Brooklyn in
the 1920s, as seen in this front page story
on the defacing of a Coney Island church.

BOTTOM

"The Mission of the Catholic Press,"
cartoon from *The Tablet*, **1930s**
Patrick Scanlan, editor of *The Tablet*, was
known for his political conservatism
and aggressive editorial style.

30
"Ss. Joachim & Anne Church, Qns. Village,"
in Chancery Parish Files, box 5, ADB.

31
"Questionnaire for a Parish History, Our
Lady of Grace, Howard Beach, June 13,
1938," Chancery Parish Files, box 7, ADB.
See also *Golden Jubilee, 1906–1956: Our
Lady of Grace R. C. Church, Howard Beach,
N.Y.* (New York, 1956), 11–12, copy in Parish
Journals, box 4, ADB. McGrath added:
"With the development of Howard Beach...
there came some bigotry. To have a Catho-
lic Church in their neighborhood meant
to devaluate their property, i.e., by bring-
ing trashy Catholics"; "Questionnaire," 3.

32
See Alden V. Brown, *The Tablet: The First
Seventy-Five Years* (Brooklyn: The Tablet,
1983), 26–27; *The New York Times*, June 1,
1927, 16. For other examples of cross burn-
ings in Queens, see *A Beacon of Light:
The Story of 75 Years, Holy Child Jesus Parish,
Richmond Hill* (New York, 1985), 29, in Parish Journals, box 4, ADB. A similar incident
occurred in Elmhurst in 1923; see www.
astorialic.org/topics/timeline/apr_p.php.

33
The Tablet, September 28, 1929, 5.

34
Day is quoted in James Terence Fisher,
*The Catholic Counterculture in America,
1933–1962* (Chapel Hill: University of North
Carolina Press, 1989), 68–69; William J.
Smith, S.J., to Rev. Francis J. McQuade, S.J.,
November 20, 1947, in Crown Heights
Labor School file, box entitled "Xavier
Labor School, 1912–1960," Archives of the
New York Province of the Society of Jesus,
New York, N.Y.

35
Fisher, *Catholic Counterculture*, 74.

36
John Gunther, *Inside U.S.A.* (New York:
Harper and Brothers, 1947), 554. For further
background, see Patrick J. McNamara.,
"A Study of the Editorial Policy of the
Brooklyn *Tablet* Under Patrick F. Scanlan,
1917–1968," M.A. thesis, St. John's Uni-
versity, 1994.

through an intermediary "because of the feeling against Catholics in the neighborhood."[30] When Father Edward McGrath took over Our Lady of Grace, Howard Beach, in 1924, local Klansmen tried to prevent him from buying land, burned crosses in front of the church, and painted the letters "KKK" across the school.[31] On Memorial Day in 1927, a riot broke out on Jamaica Avenue and Merrick Boulevard when the Klan disrupted a Knights of Columbus-sponsored parade.[32] But Catholics weren't leaving. In 1929, *Tablet* editor Patrick Scanlan wrote: "Between the Church and a successful football team there is an analogy. Both have to fight."[33]

Brooklyn Catholics, particularly the Irish, were known as a tough lot. Dorothy Day of *The Catholic Worker* complained that they "went around with a chip on their shoulder." A Jesuit working in Crown Heights during the 1940s described them as "willing to fight at the drop of a hat."[34] No one embodied this image more than Pat Scanlan, whose aggressive editorial style and unapologetic conservatism made *The Tablet* one of the most controversial news-papers of its time.[35] John Gunther called it "one of the most reactionary" in the nation.[36] Communism was Scanlan's predominant obsession: Nearly every *Tablet* issue highlighted its inroads abroad and at home. Even as Father Charles Coughlin's anticommunism descended into anti-Semitism, Scanlan praised him for saying "what millions are saying in their ordinary conversations and on the streets."[38] Long after Senator Joseph McCarthy's demise, Scanlan called him "a sterling example of an American who loved his God."[39]

But Scanlan's main audience was always Brooklyn, a place that Gunther called "a world in itself, with a fierce local nationalism."[40] By the 1940s, Brooklyn Catholicism, too, was a world in itself, with Holy Name rallies and Loyalty Day parades attracting crowds of one hundred thousand. In those pre-Internet days, novenas and parish missions, Holy Name "smokers," and Knights of Columbus councils provided standard evening fare. Parish bas-ketball tournaments were neighborhood affairs. As John McGreevey notes, the word *parish* had "a geographical as well as religious meaning."[41] "What parish are you from?" was an icebreaker.

A 1938 study of Park Slope by a Columbia University sociologist observed that the lives of the neighborhood's Catholics were "inextricably woven into the web of their religion," which determined their social contacts and acquaintances.[42] Park Slopers identified themselves from Holy Name, St. Saviour, St. Augustine, or St. Francis Xavier, to name a few parishes. East New York meant St. Rita's or St. Fortunata's for the Italians, St. Malachy's for the Irish, St. Michael's for the Germans, or St. John Cantius for the Poles. By 1920, Williamsburg was home to 14 parishes within walking distance of one another: German, Lithuanian, Polish, Italian, Ukrainian, and Irish.[43]

However, big changes were coming in the postwar years. Returning GIs had educational opportunities they could not have dreamed of before the war. Soon Catholics were moving out of the old neighborhoods into the middle class. The Depression had put a hold on suburbanization, but after the war it resumed with a vengeance. Nassau was America's fastest-growing county. Cardinal Spellman complained that half the archdiocese had moved to Queens, and he is said to have offered to trade Bishop Molloy Queens for Staten Island. If he did, Molloy had none of it.[44]

After Boston's Cardinal William H. O'Connell died in 1944, rumors abounded that Molloy would replace him. Yet Molloy once told Archbishop Richard Cushing: "When I die, I want to go directly from Brooklyn to Heaven." At his request, he was buried with a copy of *The Tablet*.[45]

Until his death in November 1956, Molloy successfully opposed Brooklyn's partition. The following April, Nassau and Suffolk were separated to form the Rockville Centre Diocese, making Brooklyn a completely urban diocese. Brooklyn and Queens experienced an influx of Hispanic and African-American residents, but, as John McGreevey notes, these transitions were not always smooth, and old-timers lamented the passing of the good old days when parish priests exhorted their flock to pray for Gil Hodges.

Yet these changes reaffirm Brooklyn Catholicism's unique character. Archbishop John Ireland summed it up nicely in an 1890 address to Brooklyn Catholics: "You hold the outposts of the continent; you are the first to greet the children of nations thronging upon our shores."[46] In 1911, Mass was celebrated in 12 languages. Almost a century later, there are 26 languages. Whether it is populated by newcomers from Ireland or Germany, Italy or Poland, the West Indies or the Jim Crow South, Puerto Rico or the Dominican Republic, Vietnam or Korea, Mexico or Nigeria, Brooklyn continues to be a "Diocese of immigrants."

37
One study estimates that during the early cold war, two thirds of its news coverage focused on Communism; see Kathleen Gefell Centola, "The American Catholic Church and Anti-Communism, 1945–1960: An Interpretive Framework and Case Studies," Ph.D. diss., SUNY Albany, 1984, 554, 546.

38
Quoted in New York *Daily News*, December 27, 1938, clipping in "Scrapbook: References, 1932–1938," Patrick Scanlan Collection, ADB.

39
The Tablet, June 15, 1957, in "Managing Editor's Obituaries, January 1953–Present," Scanlan Collection, ADB.

40
Gunther, *Inside U.S.A.*, 554.

41
McGreevey, *Parish Boundaries*, 11.

42
Christine McLaren Brown, "Social Contacts Within a Brooklyn City Block," M.A. thesis, Columbia University, 1938, 84.

43
In the Woodhaven section of Queens, 91st Avenue was the dividing line between the St. Thomas the Apostle and St. Elizabeth parishes. As late as the 1980s, it was possible to live one's entire life on either side of that avenue and have no significant interaction with Catholics who lived a block away.

44
Robert I. Gannon, S.J., *The Cardinal Spellman Story* (New York: Doubleday, 1962), 127.

45
"Archbishop Thomas Edmund Molloy," 1.

46
Rev. James H. Mitchell, ed., *Golden Jubilee Celebration of the Rt. Rev. John Loughlin, D.D., First Bishop of Brooklyn, October 18th, 1890* (Brooklyn: Golden Jubilee Committee, 1891), 142.

TOP LEFT

Knights of Columbus dedicate a new council building in Prospect Park, Brooklyn, 1925
Knights of Columbus, the Catholic lay fraternal benefit society, worked through local councils to aid those in need.

TOP RIGHT

Our Lady of Lourdes basketball team, 1936
Athletic organizations helped foster parish identity.

BOTTOM

Parish dance, 1944
Parishes sponsored a range of youth activities, including social dances.

CHURCH OF SAINT BRIDGET.

AVENUE B.

ST. BRIGID'S PARISH

A PILGRIM CHURCH FOR AN IMMIGRANT PEOPLE

Anyone hoping to enter New York's lost past faces the daunting barrier of a built-over cityscape that often thwarts our best efforts to imagine what past generations of New Yorkers saw, heard, smelled, and, of course, thought about it all.

A modern pilgrim who sets out on a journey to Catholic New York's past, on the other hand, would seem to find fewer such obstacles; Catholicism presents itself as a living artifact, a rare fixed point in an ever-shifting urban universe. Teachings, mores, customs, even Latin—the church never gets rid of anything. She is, according to the Catholic motto, *semper idem*: "always the same."

So it is that in the popular imagination Catholics arrived in New York with an Old World culture and an out-of-the-box faith, which quickly replicated itself in a network of churches that were old the moment they were built. Catholic architecture consciously evoked a distant past (usually a medieval vintage), and the Catholic faith went back farther still. *Semper idem*. Case closed.

As often happens, however, a closer inspection reveals that this impression is mostly an urban legend. Yet the truth about parish life turns out to be as compelling as the myth—and perhaps a good deal more comforting to those today who see nothing but change for the Catholic Church and assume it must be for the worse.

In fact, change has been a constant for New York City parishes. Nothing illustrates that more vividly—or poignantly—than the story of St. Brigid's parish, founded in 1848 in what is now the East Village but was known then as the Dry Dock District because of the booming shipbuilding industry on the East River. This neighborhood, spanning from Avenue B to the East River and from Houston Street north to 12th Street, was a common landing point for the masses of Irish immigrants who fled the famine of 1845 to 1851 and found work at the docks.

As the Irish population of the city swelled in the mid 19th century, there were scarcely enough churches to serve its needs. It is surprising today, given the powerhouse that is St. Patrick's Cathedral and the Irish dominance of the city's clerical ranks, to realize that there were fewer than a dozen Catholic churches in New York at the start of the 1840s, and many of those served immigrant groups other than the Irish. The Dry Dock, for example, was home to "Little Germany" because the Germans had arrived there first, en masse. The only Catholic church in the area, St. Stephen's, was for Germans, and a temporary chapel for English speakers at East 4th Street soon proved inadequate.

While conditions in the New World were little better than those left behind, most Irish Catholics spoke English, and the seminaries were soon filled with Irish priests, native and immigrant alike. These men formed the talent pool for the city's hierarchy. One of the most formidable of these leaders was New York's fourth bishop, John Hughes—known as "Dagger John" because of the slashing cross he affixed before his name as well as for his fearsome manner. Hughes was not one to let his countrymen languish in spiritual poverty, so in 1848 he ordered Father Richard Kein to build a parish for the Irish near Tompkins Square. Kein secured a parcel of land at Avenue B and 8th Street. The church was to be dedicated to St. Brigid, "the virgin saint of Erin" who heard St. Patrick himself preach.

The cornerstone for St. Brigid's church was laid by Bishop Hughes on September 10, 1848, and so great were the crowds "that some of the walls, on which they climbed to get a better view of the ceremonies, sank under their weight."[1] The building was ready for its first Mass just 15 months later, on Sunday, December 2, 1849. Credit for this swift construction went to Father Kein and to Patrick Keely, an Irish immigrant who was at the start of a career that was to make him one of the most popular church builders of the century. At a time when church finances were tight and architects were notoriously profligate, Keely could produce designs at a reasonable price and deliver them on time and at budget. By the time Keely died in 1896, he had designed some 600 churches and other sanctuaries from Canada to the Gulf of Mexico. But St. Brigid's was one of the first, and it established a familiar Keely pattern: a Gothic style with a tripartite front façade flanked by soaring bell towers. The interior featured a wide center nave under a vaulted ceiling, though in St. Brigid's the ceiling's peculiar resemblance to the inner hull of a boat was said to be the influence of the Irish

1
Rev. Patrick D. O'Flaherty, "The History of St. Brigid's Parish in the City of New York under the Administration of the Rev. Patrick F. McSweeny, 1877–1907," Ph.D. diss., Fordham University, 1952, 2.

Scene at the Irish Emigrant Office in Ann street.

TOP

Scene at the Irish Emigrant Office in Ann Street, as illustrated in *The Weekly Herald,* 1845

PAGE 54

Church of Saint Bridget, Avenue B, 1878, engraving

The parish of St. Bridget legally became St. Brigid, to follow the spelling of the parish's fifth-century Irish patroness, during the rectorship of Father Patrick F. McSweeney (1877–1907).

TOP

Scene at the Irish Emigrant Office in Ann Street, as illustrated in *The Weekly Herald,* 1845

BOTTOM

James Pringle (1788–1847), *Messrs. Smith and Company Shipyard,* 1833, oil on canvas

THE MOST REV. JOHN HUGHES, D.D.

FIRST ARCHBISHOP OF NEW YORK

"I believe, that as containing the fulness of divine revelation, the Holy Catholic Church is the only true Church on the earth although many true Catholic doctrines are found floating about, as opinions, in the religious atmosphere of protestantism." This is my Profession of Faith, of the sincerity of which the ALMIGHTY is my witness.

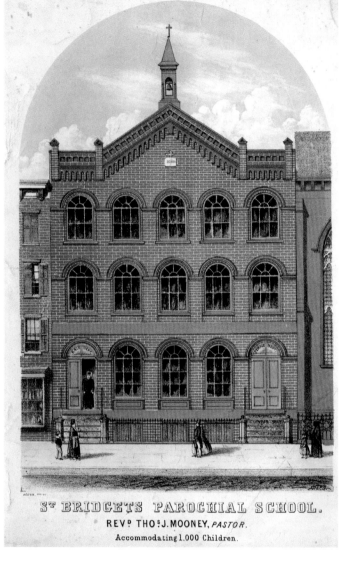

ST. BRIDGETS PAROCHIAL SCHOOL.

REVᴰ THOˢJ. MOONEY, PASTOR.

Accommodating 1,000 Children.

PREVIOUS SPREAD

Samuel B. Waugh, *Bay and Harbor of New York,* c. 1855, oil on canvas

Castle Garden on the Battery, at the left, became the immigrant registration depot in 1855, with police and agents of the Irish Emigrant Society posted at its pier to assist newcomers.

LEFT

The Most Rev. John Hughes, D.D., c. 1860, colored lithograph, published by Currier & Ives, New York

County Tyrone native John Hughes (1797–1864) actively led New York's Roman Catholics from 1842 until his death in 1864.

RIGHT

St. Bridgets Parochial School, c. 1870, colored lithograph

Christian Brothers and Sisters of Charity staffed the parish school while Rev. Thomas J. Mooney was pastor.

shipbuilders who worked on the structure (and who carved images of their faces on the capitals of some of the pillars).[2]

For all the enthusiasm that greeted the new parish, however, St. Brigid's was typical of many parishes: Money was the biggest challenge. The sepia image of working-class Catholics joining in sacrifice to establish a grandiose edifice is belied by the grim circumstances endured by many of the faithful and, by extension, much of the church in New York. Then, as today, pockets of great wealth existed alongside endemic misery. The Lower East Side, for example, was home to posh residences on Second Avenue, while from First Avenue to the river immigrants lived in squalor. The future labor leader Samuel Gompers described the "penetrating, sickening odor" of the slaughterhouses and the "nauseating" piles of decayed garbage in front of tenement buildings so unsteady that they leaned on one another for support. Many St. Brigid's parishioners gave what they could, but pastors struggled to keep the parish afloat.

The religious literacy and punctiliousness of the immigrant Irish also posed a challenge. The devout Irish Catholic of sacred memory was in many respects a recent creation. In New York in 1860, for example, Mass attendance among the Irish was still as low as 40 percent, and even those who did attend regularly were often ignorant of such basic church teachings as the Trinity. Many had to be taught fundamentals such as making the Sign of the Cross, and others had never received communion or gone to confession. "The task of the church [in New York City]," historian Jay Dolan has written, "was not only to preserve the faith of the immigrants; in many instances it was to change nominal Catholics into practicing believers."[3]

The real miracle of parishes like St. Brigid's was how well they accomplished this mission, often thanks to heroic and determined pastors. At St. Brigid's, one such priest was Father Thomas Mooney, who took over after Father Kein died of exhaustion in 1854, six years after founding the parish. Mooney immediately set to building a school, and when the Civil War broke out he served as chaplain to the legendary 69th Regiment, New York Volunteers. Yet when authorities tried to enforce conscription in July 1863, Mooney organized a neighborhood posse to repulse federal troops that were dispatched to New York to put down a weeklong draft riot, one of the deadliest civil disturbances in American history. Throughout his tenure, Mooney also worked to beautify the church, traveling to Europe and returning with French paintings of the Stations of the Cross as well as an organ with more than 1,500 pipes and a tone said to be unrivaled in any other church in the city.[4]

Mooney also tried to change what he considered the ingrained vices of his parishioners, chief among them a fondness for strong drink that often extended to the raucous funerals that became a popular trope of Irish Catholicism but a bane to priests. The clergy eventually

2
Katherine Zeltner, "Patrick Keely, Architect," *Common Bond* 15, no. 3 (spring 2000); the Keely Society (www.keelysociety.com).

3
Jay P. Dolan, "The Immigrant Church: New York's Irish and German Catholics, 1815–1865" (Baltimore: Johns Hopkins University Press, 1975), 57.

4
O'Flaherty, 6.

succeeded in bringing funerals into the sanctuary, but the wake in the pub endured. In 1866, Father Mooney founded an abstinence movement that his successors also championed, but Mooney's parishioners resisted his logic. After all, they noted that in a famous prayer dear St. Brigid herself pleaded, "I should like a great lake of beer for the King of Kings / I should like the angels of Heaven to be drinking it through time eternal."

Mooney's successor, Father Patrick McSweeney, continued to adorn the church, raising money to install chandeliers and stained-glass windows from Bavaria. An altar of carved marble and Caen stone replaced the original wooden table. At one point, the parish was the third-largest contributor of funds to the building of St. Patrick's Cathedral.[5]

Yet if this was the parish's golden age, it was, in hindsight, fairly brief. By the late 19th century, urban parishes like St. Brigid's were already facing the kinds of transformations that were to challenge them through the next century.

One source of change was the economic turmoil that hit the area's working poor hardest. By 1870, the shipyards of the Dry Dock had shut down. Some workers found jobs in the booming building industry uptown, but they often were forced to move from the neighborhood to be closer to work.

A second factor was the constantly shifting ethnic landscape—a transformation that augured many future upheavals on the East Side and elsewhere. Within a generation, the great wave of Irish immigration that had given birth to St. Brigid's already was ebbing, and by the 1870s many Irish were heading for outlying neighborhoods. (A parting irony: Due to a common misconception among the Irish in Ireland, the Irish in New York thought the saint's name was spelled "Bridget" rather than the Gaelic "Brigid." So the parish was often mistakenly known as St. Bridget's until Father McSweeney legally changed it to St. Brigid's in 1888, after many of the original Irish parishioners were gone.)

The last decade of the 19th century saw incoming streams of Southern and Eastern Europeans, including a large wave of Italians. At St. Brigid's, Father McSweeney tried to accommodate the Italians, but relations were strained. McSweeney evicted one Italian priest who brought his relatives to live with him. Moreover, while two thousand Italians came to four Masses in the basement each Sunday, McSweeney felt they were not pulling their weight financially. (St. Brigid's had paid off its debt only in 1889.) In letters to the archbishop, McSweeney complained that on one Sunday the offering plate was empty, yet "the Italians" stole the priest's new 50-dollar overcoat and breviary. The children were no better, McSweeney wrote, and could not be admitted to the parish school. "Within a month I had to expel three boys for coming, one with a loaded revolver, another with a stiletto, and a third for stabbing a pupil with a sharp pencil," he wrote.[6]

5
Ibid., 62.
6
Ibid., 74.

DEPARTURE OF THE 69ᵀᴴ REGᵗ N.Y.S.M. TUESDAY APRIL 23ᴰ 1861.
THE IRISH HEADQUARTERS AROUND Sᵗ PATRICKS CATHEDRAL, COR PRINCE & MOTT ST.

Sarony, Major & Knapp, *Departure of the 69th Regt. N.Y.S.M. Tuesday April 23rd, 1861. The Irish Headquarters Around St. Patrick's Cathedral, Cor. Prince & Mott St, for D. T. Valentine's Manual 1862*, colored lithograph
The 69th New York Regiment, a largely Irish unit, was deployed to the Virginia front in the first months of the Civil War.

Reverend Thomas J. Mooney saying Sunday Mass for the 69th Regiment of the New York State Militia, 1861
Mooney served as chaplain for the 69 Regiment, N.Y.S.M., during the first months of the Civil War.

Alexander Hatos, [St. Brigid's Roman Catholic Church], pre-1963, gelatin silver print
Tompkins Square Park faced St. Brigid's, at Avenue B and Eighth Street, in Manhattan.

Illustration depicting the New York draft riots, undated
Irish Catholics took part in the violent 1863 riots protesting the Civil War military draft.

A parish for the Italians was eventually built, but the reinvention of St. Brigid's and the neighborhood proceeded as the Irish continued to leave the parish and the community's Jewish population grew. Baptisms at St. Brigid's dropped; fewer children came to the school and fewer adults to Mass. As one biographer wrote, McSweeney "noticed these changes, but he knew there was nothing he could do to stop the march of progress. He went on ministering to his people and attempting to aid the newcomers, teaching the true Faith and administering his parish, secure in the knowledge that in all things he was doing his best."[7]

After McSweeney's death in 1907, the parish faced more difficulties. The pastor at the time was one of the most colorful priests of the day, Father Philip J. "Mac" Magrath, also known as "the Fighting Priest" because of his two-fisted defense of Irish seamen who were habitually beaten and robbed by notorious waterfront gangs like the Hudson Dusters. Magrath would roam the waterfront with a prayer book and an eight-inch rubber hose, which, he said, "drops 'em just as quick but doesn't crack the skull." In the Catholic Seamen's Mission, which Magrath ran, a sign read: "If you want to know who's boss START SOMETHING."[8]

Magrath organized a grand celebration for the parish's 75th anniversary in 1923, and worshipers thronged the Masses. Yet the observance might be viewed as the start of a long requiem. Within a few years, Mass attendance dropped to about 350, and the weekly collection was a meager 60 dollars. Enrollment fell, and the school was closed. The Great Depression nearly sealed the church's fate. Father Magrath, worn out by work and his waterfront activities, dropped dead of a heart attack in 1936, at the age of 59.[9]

Yet St. Brigid's had one more transformation in her. In the postwar era, the city built housing projects in the neighborhood that drew many newcomers, while the national and ethnic differences that had been so important in the previous century began to fade. In 1951, the parish recorded more baptisms than in any year since 1890, and hundreds of children were enrolled in catechism classes. Father Patrick D. O'Flaherty wrote in his treatise on the parish in 1952, "Ever-changing New York gives every promise of restoring the East Side as a residential section and restoring the glories of St. Brigid's, now the home of every race under heaven."[10]

It was a too hopeful vision. The neighborhood was to become desirable again, though not as O'Flaherty imagined. Even in the early 1950s, a vanguard of nouveau bohemians was arriving, with high ideals but unexpected consequences. (In 1953, William S. Burroughs took a photograph of a youthful Allen Ginsberg standing on the rooftop of his Lower East Side apartment building, framed by television antennas and the steeples of St. Brigid's.)[11] That artsy cachet eventually drew a new breed of immigrants known as yuppies, whose

7
Ibid., 79.
8
Time, August 31, 1936.
9
O'Flaherty, 117.
10
Ibid., 119.
11
Reproduced in *The New York Times Book Review,* November 19, 2006.

thirst for a cleaned-up version of the tenement experience led to sharp gentrification battles in the 1980s. Speculators quickly rebaptized the neighborhood "the East Village," to channel the hipness of Greenwich Village, and it worked.

During this time, the Catholic Church was changing as well. The Second Vatican Council introduced a new dynamic for Roman Catholicism and inspired priests at St. Brigid's to support the working poor of the area—mainly Puerto Ricans by 1960—and to announce the Church's relevancy to the area's unchurched youth. In 1967, the archdiocese designated St. Brigid's an "experimental parish" and installed a "team" of three priests "working together as equals to help break down the perception of the church as an authoritarian hierarchical structure," as the cultural historian Wayne Ashley put it. St. Brigid's original pastors would have been aghast, but the parish had no choice. In an effort to reconnect the church to the lives of the residents, the parish sponsored block parties and opened the rectory to drug addicts and troubled youth. They moved the Spanish Mass from the basement to the main sanctuary, added Puerto Rican flourishes to the liturgy, and most notably staged the Stations of the Cross outside on Good Friday, often using neighborhood blights as contemporary stand-ins for the tribulations of Jesus.[12] Yet clashes were inevitable. Old-timers who were not Hispanic opposed the changes, and there were few Latino clerics to help out. Efforts to "update" the Mass by including songs like "Age of Aquarius" from the pop musical *Hair* were met with derision.

Eventually the Puerto Ricans moved out, the yuppies moved in, and the 1990s were marked by declines so steep that in early 2007, despite vocal opposition by a remnant of supporters, the Archdiocese of New York closed St. Brigid's for good.

Perhaps such an ending was inevitable. Even those famous Keely steeples that had drawn untold souls to Mass across the decades were always problematic, requiring periodic restorations. In 1963, the steeples had been brought down, forever diminishing the old church's grand façade. That was a decade after they had framed Allen Ginsberg and just a year after the Irish-American poet Frank O'Hara wrote an ode, "Weather near St. Brigid's Steeples," which spoke of the towers "so beautiful and trusting / lying there on the sky."

St. Brigid's, "the Famine church," was born out of hardship and was defined by struggle and change. And maybe that's how St. Brigid's should be remembered. Rather than promote the pleasing idea of St. Brigid's—or any parish—as the final triumph of Catholic New York, it may be more realistic, and consoling, to reimagine St. Brigid's as an emblem of the pilgrim church and her pilgrim people, whose journey through this world, and on to the world to come, is never at an end.

12
Wayne Ashley, "Stations of the Cross: Christ, Politics, and Processions on New York's Lower East Side," in *Gods of the City: Religion and the Urban American Landscape,* ed. Robert A. Orsi (Bloomington: Indiana University Press, 1999), 345ff.
13
The Collected Poems of Frank O'Hara (New York: Alfred A. Knopf, 1971), 430.

LEFT
St. Brigid's School Children's Chalice with presentation inscription to Archbishop John Hughes, 1859
In 1862, Archbishop Hughes presented this 19th-century Italian silver gilt chalice to the Children of St. Brigid's School.

TOP RIGHT
Donald Greenhaus, *Watching an Argument in Tompkins Square Park*, 1960s
Tomkins Square Park became a counter-culture haven in the 1960s.

BOTTOM RIGHT
James Estrin, [Demolition of Saint Brigid's], as seen in *The New York Times*, July 28, 2006

ALEX STOROZYNSKI

FROM SERFDOM TO FREEDOM

POLISH CATHOLICS FIND A REFUGE

1

Norman Davies, *God's Playground: A History of Poland,* vol. 1 (New York: Columbia University Press, 1982).

There was no greater moment for New York's Polish Catholics than when Karol Wojtyła, the cardinal-archbishop of Krakow, was elected Pope in 1978. My mother's jaw dropped, and the dish towel she was holding fell to the floor as our TV beamed images of a cherub-faced Pole waving from the Vatican balcony. The following year, when Wojtyła, now Pope John Paul II, visited Battery Park to give a speech about freedom, my mother stood in the rain for hours to hear him. When he finally arrived, hundreds of immigrants began chanting in Polish, "Long live the Pope."

Deep in the multitude, my mother cried out, "Long live Poland!"

The Pontiff stopped in his tracks, turned, and parted his way through the crowd.

He took my mother by the hand, looked into her eyes, and said, "Long live Poland."

At the time, of course, Poland was trapped behind the Iron Curtain; during that warm handshake, two people who had suffered through the destruction and occupation of their homeland by the Nazis and the Soviets expressed hope that someday Poland would again be free.

For Polish Catholics in New York, nationality and religious faith were intertwined. That was true during the Middle Ages; it remained true centuries later, when a Polish Pope and a Polish immigrant met in Battery Park.[1]

Polish Catholic immigrants to New York brought with them customs and traditions that were quite different from those of the Irish and Germans who preceded them. Instead of birthdays, Slavs were obsessed with celebrating "name's day," the holidays of the saints in whose honor they named their children. On Christmas Eve, they shared *Opłatek*, the eucharist, among themselves in their own homes before sitting down to dinners of borscht and fish. On Easter Monday, Polish children celebrated *Smigus Dyngus*, as boys doused girls with buckets of water to commemorate the baptism of the first Polish king, Mieszko, on Easter Monday in 966. And they were devoted to their national icon, the Black Madonna of Czestochowa.

Poles who settled permanently in New York made up one of the poorest, least educated, and most disorganized immigrant groups. Those who had some money saw Manhattan as a launching pad to cities further inland, such as Chicago, Detroit, and Milwaukee. The first Polish parish in America was founded not in New York but in Galveston, Texas, in 1854.[2]

Many Poles who came to America before the Civil War had been serfs, so they instinctively opposed slavery. When the war broke out and Abraham Lincoln asked for volunteers for the Union Army, Wlodzimierz Krzyzanowski (1824–1887), a cousin of Polish composer Frederic Chopin, started a "Polish legion" in New York City to fight for the North. Krzyzanowski (which means "bearer of the cross") moved quickly up the ranks to colonel. But, according to German-American statesman Carl Schurz, when Lincoln nominated Krzyzanowski as a brigadier general, the Senate failed to confirm him "because there was nobody there who could pronounce his name."[3]

Eventually, Lincoln's promotion of Krzyzanowski was approved by brevet, meaning that he had limited use of the higher rank. Poles saw Krzyzanowski's predicament as typical of their experience in America, although after the war Krzyzanowski served in a number of federal posts, including that of special agent in New York's Custom House. Many Poles feared that their language, culture, and religion were getting lost in translation. For better or worse, issues of politics, religion, and culture were intertwined for Polish Catholics. The Church as an institution was their great defender, but in postbellum New York the Poles did not have a church of their own.

By the 1870s, there were about 2,000 Polish Catholics living in Manhattan. They opened their own butcher shops, with kielbasa and hams hanging in the windows, they printed Polish-language newspapers, and they ran their own factories. But they wanted their own place to pray. In March 1874, Father Wojciech Mielcuszny arrived in New York to help the Poles establish a parish of their own. The following year, he wrote in the *Polish Catholic Gazette*, "Why is it that New York, which has the first and largest Polish immigrant settlement, does not have a Polish church? What are the reasons for this chaos? It's that our

2
Charles G. Herbermann, Edward A. Pace, Conde B. Pallen, Thomas J. Shahan, John J. Wynne, eds., *The Catholic Encyclopedia: An International Work of Reference on the Constitution, Doctrine, Discipline, and History of the Catholic Church*, 15 vols. (New York: Encyclopedia Press, 1913), 205.

3
Carl Schurz, *The Reminiscences of Carl Schurz*, vol. 2 (Garden City, N.Y.: Doubleday, Page, 1917), 407.

Shea Stadium, Queens, October 3, 1979

The scoreboard read "POPE!" as Pope John
Paul II (1920–2005) greeted the crowds
"from Long Island—and New Jersey—and
Connecticut—and Broke-leen."

**Pope John Paul II at Shea Stadium,
Queens, October 3, 1979**

More than 50,000 rain-soaked people
cheered the Pope as he addressed the
crowd in four languages—English,
Spanish, Italian, and Polish.

71

CHURCH OF SAINT STANISLAUS.
STANTON STREET.

TOP LEFT

Colonel Wlodzimierz Krzyzanowski, c. 1864
Krzyzanowski (1824–1887) led the 58th New York Infantry Regiment (the "Polish Legion") as it fought for the Union from 1861–1865.

TOP RIGHT

St. Stanislaus on Stanton Street, engraving, from John Gilmary Shea, editor, *The Catholic Churches of New York City*, 1878
St. Stanislaus was the first Polish Catholic church in the Archdiocese of New York.

BOTTOM

Fourth grade class at St. Stanislaus Kostka School, Greenpoint, Brooklyn, 1915
The parish was founded for Polish immigrants in 1896 and remains the largest Polish-language Catholic church in greater New York.

brothers who have settled in New York are those who do not have the funds to move further into this country." [4]

Father Mielcuszny began a fundraising campaign and collected enough money to buy some land. New York Poles enlisted the help of an erudite count, Piotr Leliwa Wodzicki, to ask Archbishop John McCloskey for permission to open their own parish.

Count Wodzicki began his presentation for McCloskey in Latin, but he switched to English after McCloskey said he could not converse in Latin. The count explained that his countrymen wanted to build their own church. According to Father Waclaw Kruszka, an early 20th-century historian of Polish America, McCloskey replied: "The Poles can use a pig shanty as their church." [5] Whether McCloskey actually made such a statement or not, the fact that Poles like Father Kruszka believed that he did indicates the level of suspicion between the Irish-dominated church hierarchy and the newly arriving Poles. In any case, Father Mielcuszny built a wooden church at 318 Henry Street on the Lower East Side, where the first Polish Mass was said on December 6, 1875. The wooden church was packed with proud Poles who wanted to pray aloud in their own language. Once they had their own house of worship, the Poles began leaving more in the collection plate, and two and a half years later the parish had enough money to purchase a former Presbyterian church on Stanton Street and convert it into a Polish Catholic church. [6]

The Poles were building churches in Brooklyn as well. According to the files of Monsignor John K. Sharp, a pastor and historian of the Brooklyn Diocese, there were about one hundred Polish families in Brooklyn by the 1870s, and in 1875 they opened St. Casimir's church in Fort Greene. [7] With the sanctuary that this church provided them, thousands more Poles settled in Brooklyn, which was then still a separate city.

Brooklyn's bishop, Charles E. McDonnell, decided that "the best way to look after [the Poles] was to establish separate houses of worship." [8] McDonnell was concerned about Polish dissatisfaction with the church, concluding that separate parishes would keep them within the flock. He welcomed Polish parishes, leading to the opening of St. John Cantius church in East New York in 1903, Our Lady of Czestochowa in South Brooklyn in 1904, and the largest Polish church in New York, St. Stanislaus Kostka, in Greenpoint. The parish was established in 1896, and the church opened in 1904.

The Poles had a rude awakening in the early 1900s, when they began to open parochial schools that taught Polish language and arts classes, in addition to offering religious instruction. Bishops in the New York archdiocese frowned on Polish classes in parish schools because the hierarchy was trying to encourage integration into the larger community, rather than self-segregation and isolation. The breaking point came when the Church hierarchy

4
Rev. Wacław Kruszka, *Historya polska w Ameryce: poczatek, wzrost i rozwój dziejowy osad polskich w Północnej Ameryce* [The history of Poland in America: The beginning, growth, and historic development of Polish settlements in North America] (Milwaukee, Wis.: Drukiem Spolki Wdawniczej Kuryera, 1908), 182.

5
Kruszka, *Historya polska*, 183.

6
Kruszka, *Historya polska*, 183.

7
Danuta Piatkowska, *Polskie Koscioly w Nowym Jorku* [Polish churches in New York] (New York: Opole, 2002), 271.

8
The Brooklyn Standard Union, July 1910.

TOP

Graduating class, Holy Cross School, Maspeth, Queens, 1917

BOTTOM

Congregation of the Polish National Catholic Church of Resurrection, Greenpoint, Brooklyn, 1940s

Pulaski Day parade, Manhattan, 1939

The Marje Konopnick Dance Group of
PNCC of Resurrection on the church
steps, c. 1939

told the Poles that it owned their churches, not the local parishes—an echo of a controversy over trusteeship that had occurred during the reign of Bishop John Hughes. The Poles, stunned, demanded their own bishop.

Polish parishes in other parts of the country were experiencing similar pains—as were other, non-English-speaking Catholic groups. Some Polish priests were so disillusioned that in 1897 they founded the Polish National Catholic Church in Scranton, Pennsylvania, and named Father Franciszek Hodur as their bishop.[9]

The creation of this schismatic sect was a wake-up call for the American Catholic Church, which feared that other ethnic groups might also break away. The Catholic hierarchy became more accommodating, and in the early 20th century Polish bishops were named in Chicago, Detroit, and Milwaukee.[10] One of the driving forces for change was Reverend Waclaw Kruszka, an activist priest and historian of Polish immigrants in America. In an article entitled "Polyglot Bishops for Polyglot Dioceses" in the July 29, 1901, edition of the *New York Freeman's Journal*, Father Kruszka demanded that Poles be included in the church's hierarchy.[11]

Archbishop Michael Augustine Corrigan of the New York archdiocese worked to smooth out the rocky relationship that Cardinal McCloskey had with the Poles. In an 1891 trip to the Vatican, Corrigan met Father Jozef Dworzak, who was obtaining his doctorate in theology at Gregorian University in Rome. In 1894, Corrigan invited Dworzak to New York, and the two formed a close bond. Dworzak spent the next 57 years in the inner circle of the New York Archdiocese, helping to spur a building boom of Polish churches and parochial schools in the first half of the 20th century.[12] In all, Poles built 19 churches during the height of their presence in the five boroughs. But, like other Catholic ethnic groups, the Poles began to exit the city after World War II, leaving behind evidence of their piety and their devotion to their homeland.

New York's Poles never got the bishop they hoped for, but after the election of Karol Wojtyła as Pope, they welcomed to New York the new bishop of Rome, a fellow countryman, a man who embodied Polish devotion to church and nationality.

9 Frank Spencer Mead, *Handbook of Denominations in the United States* (Nashville: Abingdon Press, 1965), 172; Piatkowska, *Polskie Koscioly*, 33.
10 Joseph J. Parot, *Polish Catholics in Chicago, 1850–1920: A Religious History* (Dekalb, Ill.: Northern Illinois University Press, 1981).
11 Rev. Wacław Kruszka, *Siedm siedmioleci, czyli półwieku życia: pamiętnik i przyczynek do historji polskie w Ameryce* [Seven septennials, or half a century of life, memoirs, and contributions of the history of Poles in America] (Milwakuee, Wis.: Poznan, 1924), 386.
12 Piatkowska, *Polskie Koscioly*, 96–97.

RIGHT
Religji Rzymsko-Katolickiej Nr. 2, [a Polish-language edition of the Baltimore Catechism], published by W. H. Sadlier, Inc., New York, 1935–36

BOTTOM
Pennant celebrating October 1995 visit of Pope John Paul II to United States and New York, silk-screened felted paper A Central Park papal mass on October 7, 1995, attended by more than 125,000 people, highlighted Pope John Paul II's second visit to New York.

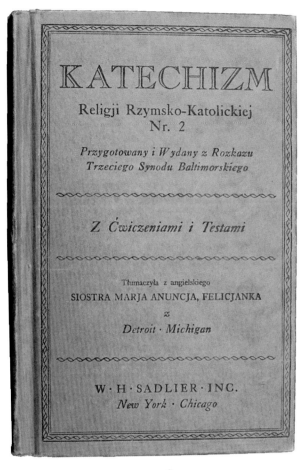

J. Schmitt, *Bird's Eye View of Calvary Cemetery* (New York: P. Stutzman, publisher; printed by Endicott & Co., 1855)
Museum of the City of New York, J. Clarence Davies Collection, 34.100.24

BUILDING CATHOLIC NEW YORK: INSTITUTIONS AND ORGANIZATIONS

RAIL ROAD CROSSING
LOOK OUT FOR THE CARS.

Mother Frances Xavier Cabrini, c. 1880

The Sweetness of a Sunday Gathering

On July 20, 1907, Mother Frances X. Cabrini sent the following letter to Leone Reynaudi, the commissioner general of emigration for the Italian government. Mother Cabrini hoped to obtain additional subsidies from the Italian government for her work with Italian Catholic immigrants in New York and elsewhere. In this excerpt from her letter, she describes the work of her order, the Missionary Sisters of the Sacred Heart, in building institutions to serve poor Catholics. She paid particular emphasis on Columbus Hospital in Manhattan.

In all the schools established by me in the United States, besides courses of study prescribed by the government, our language is taught by Italian sisters. The teaching, books and stationery are all free for children enrolled in our schools.

In the orphanages are gathered Italian girls who have lost their parents in work-related accidents or misfortune. These youngsters are taught our beautiful language and they are instructed in domestic arts and crafts which will enable them to earn an honest living. The youths, numbering approximately 5,000 who find asylum and education in our schools and orphanages, learn to know and love our native land.

Columbus Hospital in New York is exclusively Italian. Of the 1,355 patients treated in 1905, according to the latest report...90 percent were Italian. The few non-Italians were emergency cases which we could not refuse, or paying patients who were admitted to help defray expenses for the free patients. How efficacious was the care administered to our compatriots by our sisters, who know their eating habits and serve food according to their taste, is shown by the low mortality rate....

The dispensary connected with the hospital has given proof of great vitality. During the past year about 5,000 Italians received free medical treatment; 22,000 were medically examined; 22,400 prescriptions were filled out for them, and 10,500 received surgical care....

Mother Cabrini went on to describe the religious and community life of an Italian parish in Manhattan.

To the school there is united a church, which in various cities serves as a parish for the Italians. The one on 150th Street, New York City, has four or five Masses every Sunday with a fine attendance by our people. Only a person who has lived far from their country, separated from the most precious domestic joys...can value the sweetness that lies in the Sunday gathering of our workers who hurry to us in their best attire. There they hear a good word, which will animate them in their struggle for existence; there, reunited in the courtyard of the house after Mass, as they once did in the square of their own village church, entertaining their compatriots, they forget for a little while the distance from their native land. There, in the afternoon, the young people get together for recreation, and the various societies of women and men come in turn to spend an hour or two.

It follows that the rapport between the sisters and the various colonies is most friendly; there is no public or domestic need in which the Italians do not have recourse to the sisters. Especially in times of an epidemic, when the doctor and the priest were forbidden to enter the houses of our conationals for fear of contamination...a sister was always welcome at the bedside of those dying of yellow fever; when assured that the victim's children would be care for by the sisters, the victim expired peacefully.

I have the pleasure of adding that the above works not only compare with those of other nations, but that they are an honor to the Italian name because of the importance they have assumed among American institutions....

EMIGRANT *INDUSTRIAL* SAVINGS BANK

TYLER ANBINDER

SAVING GRACE

THE EMIGRANT SAVINGS BANK
AND ITS DEPOSITORS

1

Entry for account Number 1, Test Books,
Emigrant Industrial Savings Bank Papers,
New York Public Library; Seventh Ward,
First District, p. 237, 1850 manuscript
U.S. Census returns, National Archives
(both accessed via Ancestry.com). For a
more detailed and nuanced account of
the bank's founding, see Marion Casey,
"Refractive History: Memory and the
Founders of the Emigrant Savings
Bank," in Casey and J. J. Lee, eds., *Making
the Irish American: History and Heritage
of the Irish in the United States* (New
York, 2006), 319.

Bridget White must have been both nervous and excited on September 30, 1850, as the tall
wooden doors were flung open and she strode to the counter, at the head of the line, to open
the very first account at the new savings bank at 51 Chambers Street, directly behind City
Hall and less than half a mile from her Henry Street apartment. The 27-year-old White, who
had immigrated to New York six years earlier, would have been nervous because she carried
with her one hundred dollars, the equivalent of about $2,500 today, a sum that was most
likely the bulk of her family's savings. But White would have been excited as well, and not
only because she left the counter clutching the first passbook issued by the new institution:
Before she exited, who should enter to open his own account but the Right Reverend John
Hughes, bishop of New York. For the bank at which White had opened her account was no
ordinary bank, but the Emigrant Industrial Savings Bank, an institution that Hughes and
some of New York's leading Irish businessmen had founded to cater to the financial needs
of the tens of thousands of Irish Catholic immigrants like White who poured annually into
the port of New York during the mid 19th century.[1]

The Emigrant Savings Bank was an outgrowth of the Irish Emigrant Society, which had
been founded in 1840 in order to assist Irish immigrants with settling in America, finding
a job, and sending remittances back to Ireland. The bank itself was chartered by the New
York State Legislature in April 1850. In its first half-dozen years, the Emigrant grew rapidly,
so that by 1856 its approximately 11,000 accounts held more than $1,300,000. This level
of business placed the Emigrant in the middle range of New York's 14 or so savings banks,

well behind the largest, such as the Bleecker (with 35,000 accounts and $9 million in assets) and the Bowery (55,000 accounts and $7 million in assets), but ahead of the Dry Dock, the East River, and the Sixpenny. The Emigrant in this period conducted business from ten o'clock in the morning until two in the afternoon and again from five in the evening until seven, six days a week. It operated at first out of rented rooms, but by 1857 the institution could afford to buy its Chambers Street location and build its own "elegant iron banking house" with a façade "painted in imitation of Caen stone."[2]

The Emigrant eventually became one of New York's best-known savings banks; its early history is noteworthy because the motives underlying its creation reflect how wide the gulf was between Irish Catholic immigrants and native New Yorkers. After all, there were many other savings banks at which the newcomers could have opened accounts, including several just a few blocks from the Emigrant. But the records of the Emigrant tell us far more. Balance ledgers from the very first accounts there have survived, allowing us to track the financial successes and failures of immigrants such as Bridget White in remarkable detail. Just as important is the survival of the bank's "test books," so called because they contained detailed biographical information about each depositor and his or her relatives, so that those who sought to withdraw funds could be quizzed to verify their identities. The Emigrant's records therefore offer a variety of important insights into the lives of Catholic New Yorkers in the era of the Irish Famine and the American Civil War.

Bank records such as Emigrant's also provide fascinating details concerning the employment opportunities available for the Famine-era immigrants. The ten most common occupations followed by the Emigrant's predominantly Irish-born depositors before the Civil War were (in descending order of popularity): day laborer, domestic servant, clerk, tailor, shoemaker, porter, priest, peddler, carpenter, and seamstress.[3] It makes perfect sense that there were more laborers and domestics among the depositors than members of any other occupational group, because those were the jobs Irish immigrant men and women, respectively, took most commonly upon arrival in America. Indeed, six of the ten most popular occupations among the Emigrant's depositors also appear on the top-ten list of depositor occupations for six of New York's leading savings banks that was published in the New York Herald in 1857.

2
O'Grada, "The Famine, The New York Irish and Their Bank," 228–29; New York Herald, October 13, 1857, p. 2; The New York Times, October 4, 1853, p. 6, and May 12, 1857, p. 8.

3
Occupational data based on occupations listed in the EISB Test Books, NYPL. My rankings are based on a random sampling of nine hundred of the first eighteen thousand accounts opened at the EISB from September 1850 until October 1858.

PAGE 82

Emigrant Industrial Savings Bank, c. 1860
This structure housed the bank at
51 Chambers Street, Manhattan, from
1858 to 1885.

LEFT

Irish emigrants leaving Queenstown,
Ireland, for New York, wood engraving
reproduced in *Harper's Weekly*,
September 26, 1874

RIGHT

The Lament of the Irish Emigrant sheet
music with poetry by the Hon. Mrs.
Price Blackwood and music by William
R. Dempster, published by Geo. P. Reed,
Boston, 1843
Irish Gaelic speakers often described
their migration in terms of banishment,
exile, or homesickness.

BOTTOM

Ladies admission ticket to First Annual
Ball of the Irish Emigrant Society, 1845
From its founding in 1840, the Irish
Emigrant Society provided settlement
assistance to new arrivals.

Most Common Occupations of Account Holders at EISB versus Those at Other Top New York Banks[4]

EMIGRANT BANK, 1850–1858		SIX LEADING NEW YORK BANKS, 1856	
1	Laborers	1	Domestic Servants
2	Domestic Servants	2	Boardinghouse Keepers
3	Clerks	3	Tailors
4	Tailors	4	Laborers
5	Shoemakers	5	Clerks
6	Porters	6	Seamstresses
7	Priests	7	Grocers
8	Peddlers	8	Carpenters
9	Carpenters	9	Storekeepers
10	Seamstresses	10	Manufacturers

The discrepancies in the two lists offer insight into the differences between New York's Catholic community and its non-Catholic population in the 1850s. Among the occupations that do not appear on the Emigrant list but are found on the all-New York list are better-paying ones such as grocer, storekeeper, and manufacturer. In their place we find peddlers, porters, and shoemakers—what one would imagine to be some of the lowest-paying occupations in the city. Finally, the prominent place of Roman Catholic priests among the Emigrant's depositors is noteworthy, though these accounts were often ones in which the pastors kept parish funds in trust. Nonetheless, that so many priests opened accounts at the Emigrant indicates the extent to which Catholic leaders perceived the institution to be *their* bank and likewise reflects the priests' efforts to set an example of savings and thriftiness for their parishioners.

The records of the Emigrant also illuminate the more conservative manner in which Irish Catholic immigrants defined gender roles in their families. At the Bleecker, the savings bank with more assets than any other in New York, women held the vast majority of the accounts. Not only did single women open three times as many accounts there as single men, but more than three quarters of the accounts opened by married persons were opened in the name of the wife only. In 19th-century America, women typically controlled the family purse strings, budgeting money for food, rent, fuel, and other expenses. At the Emigrant, in contrast, two thirds of the accounts opened by married persons were opened in the husband's name only. A quarter were opened in the wife's name only, and the remainder were joint accounts. The differences between the Bleecker and the Emigrant account holders probably reflect the Irish immigrants' more conservative views concerning the role women should take in family financial planning.[5]

4
EISB statistics based on database described in n. 3. The data on the other banks come from the New York *Herald*, October 31, 1857, p. 2. The six banks whose depositors composed this list are the Bowery, Bleecker, Manhattan, Greenwich, Irving, and the EISB. The Bowery and Bleecker depositors probably account for three quarters of the depositors whose occupations were tallied.

5
EISB statistics based on database described in n. 3. Bleecker Savings Bank data from New York *Herald*, October 31, 1857, p. 2.

"Women depositors of The Emigrant Savings Bank withdrawing money to send to their suffering relatives in the Old Country," *Frank Leslie's Illustrated*, March 13, 1880

Stanley Fox, *The Labor Exchange—Interior View of the Office*, published in *Harper's Weekly*, August 15, 1868

New York State operated a Labor Exchange at Castle Garden to assist immigrants seeking jobs with reputable employers at agreed-upon wages.

TOP LEFT

Emigrant Industrial Savings Bank,
Pay Tellers Department, 1893

TOP RIGHT

Emigrant Industrial Savings Bank,
Chambers Street headquarters, 1913,
gelatin silver print

BOTTOM

Statement of the Emigrant Industrial
Savings Bank depicting its Chambers
Street headquarters, 1901

FOLLOWING SPREAD

McSpedon & Baker, *Five Points*, 1847,
lithograph, published in *D. T. Valentine's
Manual 1855*

The Five Points district in the heart of the
Sixth Ward, home to many Irish Catholic
immigrants, was reputedly the worst
slum in the nation in the mid 19th century.
Many of Emigrant Industrial Savings
Bank's early customers lived in this
neighborhood.

The Emigrant account books also indicate that Irish Catholic immigrants of the Famine era were able to save far more money than historians have previously imagined. For many decades, a deep pessimism has pervaded the literature on the Famine immigrants. Any significant improvement in their circumstances, such studies have implied, came in the lives of their assimilated children. There are exceptions, but most scholars continue to believe, as Oscar Handlin put it more than 50 years ago, that the Famine Irish were both economically and socially "fated to remain a massive lump in the community, undigested, undigestible."[6] Yet in Emigrant accounts opened from 1850 to 1858, the median initial deposit was $70, the equivalent of about $1,700 today. The median high balance in each depositor's account reached $203 ($5,000 today). Some of the immigrants did very well, as the average high balance ultimately achieved by the bank's depositors was $494, or about $12,000 in modern terms.[7]

One factor that determined the success with which the Emigrant's depositors accumulated wealth was how long they had been in America. Those who arrived in the United States before 1845 had substantially higher account balances than those who had arrived more recently (an average of $475 for the pre-Famine immigrants versus $249 for the Famine-era ones). Still, both sums are impressive.

Another variable that determined the ability to save was occupation. For example, female domestic servants were able to save far more than seamstresses, perhaps because domestics typically received room and board in addition to their small salaries (though a surprisingly large number of EISB domestics did not live where they worked). Domestics on average were able to save $201 in their accounts, versus only $114 for seamstresses. That domestics were typically unmarried while seamstresses were usually married (or widowed) with children must have affected their relative abilities to save.

Among men, laborers were able to save on average $196 (nearly $5,000 today), a surprisingly high figure given that workers in that field faced frequent furloughs and unemployment. Carpenters, in contrast—skilled tradesmen who ought to have earned significantly more than laborers—in fact saved slightly less. Perhaps Irish immigrants found it difficult to break into the carpentry trade in America and thus may have been discriminated against in pay or even found it hard to acquire work. Peddlers, in contrast, saved far more than one might expect. Their high balances averaged $365 (about $9,000 today).

One might wonder how representative the EISB customers were. Perhaps they were the exceptions within the Irish immigrant community, or immigrants who arrived in America with savings in hand, and therefore their accounts tell us little about how Famine-era immigrants really lived. But even if one looks solely at a group of depositors who we know arrived

6
Oscar Handlin, *Boston's Immigrants: A Study in Acculturation* (1941; rev. ed., Cambridge, Mass., 1959), 55.

7
These and all subsequent data concerning the savings of EISB depositors is from the database described in n. 3. To calculate the 2007 value of EISB balances, I multiplied 1850 dollars by 24.60, as suggested by the U.S. Department of Labor's *Handbook of Labor Statistics*, available at http://minneapolisfed.org/research/data/us/calc/hist1800.cfm.

in New York destitute and in terrible health at the height of the Famine, we find similar results. In the impoverished Five Points neighborhood of New York, for example, there lived a large concentration of immigrants who had been shipped out of Ireland by their landlord, the Marquis of Lansdowne, in 1851 with virtually nothing but the clothes on their backs. We know from eyewitnesses both in Ireland and New York that they arrived without savings and near starvation. Yet the Lansdowne immigrants were determined savers, and about half of the adults among them who lived in Five Points opened accounts at the Emigrant. Working overwhelmingly as laborers, domestics, and washers, each Lansdowne immigrant saved, on average, $200. Some managed to accumulate the modern equivalent of $10,000 or even $15,000 before they had been in New York even a decade, a remarkable achievement.[8]

Another immigrant who managed to save such impressive sums was Bridget White. She and her husband, Richard, both worked long hours with needle and thread in their dark, fetid apartment in the rear building at 45 Henry Street. In 1850, when they opened their joint account, they shared their cramped quarters with their three small American-born children—five-year-old Eliza, three-year-old William, and one-year-old Sarah. To enable them to save, they took in boarders as well, an Irish-immigrant carpenter and his wife.[9]

Slowly but surely, the Whites added to the hundred dollars that they had entrusted to the Emigrant in September 1850, making three to six deposits per year and resisting the temptation to make even a single withdrawal during the first five years they had the account. By January 1856, just before Bridget gave birth to her fourth child, Mary, the Whites had accumulated $633.07 in their account, about $15,000 today.

Like many of the Famine-era immigrants, the Whites decided to use their savings to escape the crowded city. Sometime soon after they closed their account at the Emigrant in September 1856, the Whites moved west to the town of Bloomington, Illinois. There they were able to buy their own home while continuing to work as tailors. Bridget had three more children, and by 1870 their real estate was valued at an impressive $6,000. The Whites' story, however, was not one of unconstrained upward mobility. While Richard and Bridget's eldest son, William, became an iron molder, the two younger boys worked as "horseshoers" in Bloomington well into the 20th century.[10]

Still, the White family, like the Lansdowne immigrants and so many others who opened accounts at the Emigrant Savings Bank, improved their circumstances significantly in a remarkably short period of time. New York and the rest of the United States offered economic opportunities for hardworking men and women that could hardly be imagined for most Catholics in Ireland. The story of the Emigrant Savings Bank and its depositors helps explain why, despite the many hardships that the Famine emigrants faced, New York and its growing economy remained such magnet to them throughout the 19th century and beyond.

8
Tyler Anbinder, "From Famine to Five Points: Lord Lansdowne's Irish Tenants Encounter North America's Most Notorious Slum," *American Historical Review* 107 (April 2002): 351–87.

9
Seventh Ward, First District, p. 237, 1850 manuscript U.S. Census returns, National Archives.

10
Entry for account Number 1, Account Ledgers, Emigrant Industrial Savings Bank Papers, New York Public Library; First Ward, City of Bloomington, McLean Co., Ill., p. 152, 1860 manuscript U.S. Census returns; City of Bloomington, p. 46, 1870 manuscript U.S. Census returns; City of Bloomington, Enum. Dist. 169, pp. 23, 49, 1880 manuscript U.S. Census returns; Sixth Ward, City of Bloomington, Enum. Dist. 91, p. 7, 1900 manuscript U.S. Census returns; City of Bloomington, Sixth Ward, Enum. Dist. 91, p. 7B, 1910 manuscript U.S. Census returns; City of Bloomington, Enum. Dist. 93, p. 8B, 1920 manuscript U.S. Census returns, National Archives.

BERNADETTE McCAULEY

APART AND AMONG

SISTERS IN THE LIVES OF CATHOLIC NEW YORKERS

1

Ira Glackens, *William Glackens and the Eight* (New York: Horizon Press, 1957), 79; Richard J. Wattenmaker, "The Art of William Glackens," Ph.D. diss., New York University, 1972, xv, 55.

A spring edition of *Collier's* magazine in 1910 included a delightful drawing by the New York artist William Glackens. It's an energetic scene of Washington Square Park bustling with activity, and in the far right corner, just past the statue of the Italian hero Garibaldi, two nuns walk purposely amid the crowd. The sisters blend in and stand out at the same time—just two more New Yorkers among many others but distinguished by their distinctive dress, apparent even in a black-and-white illustration. In this image, Glackens, who lived on the square, acknowledged something that has too often been forgotten in the history of New York City, as it was for a long time in the history of American Catholicism: Nuns—more accurately "sisters," or "women religious" in contemporary language—were a familiar part of the landscape in New York for a very long time.[1]

For a good part of the 19th and 20th centuries, sisters were very active participants in the interrelated worlds of education, health care, and social welfare in the city. Their involvement in the development of Catholicism in New York and the concurrent role of the Church in those areas was enormous. Numbers alone do not sufficiently illustrate the importance of understanding sisters' involvement, but they are revealing: By the end of the 19th century, more than 2,000 women were living in sisterhoods in the Archdiocese of New York and the Diocese of Brooklyn. While they had chosen a life in a religious community separate from the rest of the world, they were also women actively engaged in the life of the city through their work as nurses, teachers, and founders and managers of hospitals, orphanages, and homes for the elderly. In this work, they lessened some of the harsher aspects

Designed & Drawn on Stone by Hoffy

MARIA MONK,
Taken from Life
FATHER PHELAN and LITTLE PHELAN.
Published by
Bowen & Hoffy, 59 Cedar Street.

PAGE 94
William J. Glackens (1870–1938), *A Spring Morning in Washington Square, New York*
This drawing was published in black and white in *Collier's* on April 16, 1910.

LEFT
A. Hoffy, *Maria Monk, Taken from Life, Father Phelan and Little Phelan,* **1836, lithograph published by Bowen & Hoffy**
The 1836 publication of Maria Monk's book *Awful Disclosures of the Hotel Dieu Nunnery of Montreal,* a fictional account of convent life, fueled increased anti-Catholicism and made the author perhaps the best-known ex-nun in America.

RIGHT
The Sisters School [Sisters of Charity], **engraved frontispiece published in Mrs. J. Sadlier [Mary Ann Sadlier],** *The Blakes and Flanagans: A Tale, Illustrative of Irish Life in the United States,* **1865**
The Sisters of Charity, who wore a distinctive bonnet based on that worn by their foundress St. Elizabeth Seton, instructed girls in many New York parochial schools.

THE SISTERS SCHOOL.—PAGE 111.

of urban life for many New Yorkers and participated in the creation of a new landscape of urban services.[2]

Success in their work was in no way guaranteed; beginnings were precarious, and a new foundation of sisters needed the support of friends. In fact, the first effort, an Ursuline foundation in 1812, didn't work out. Unlike Boston Ursulines, who were burned out of their convent, these sisters made their own choice to leave because, among other problems, they were unable to attract recruits—"postulants" in religious language—who would be a critical factor for a foundation's success. (Like the Boston Ursulines, these sisters were quite successful in attracting students, many non-Catholics among them, whose parents wanted a convent education for their daughters.)

Five years later, another group, the Sisters of Charity from the Maryland community founded by New York–born Elizabeth Seton (1774–1821), came, stayed, and—as it might be said of so many sisterhoods—conquered. Fifty years later, the community included more than 800 professed sisters and had a healthy novitiate. Their efforts were emblematic of others that followed and were integral to the survival of the Catholic immigrant communities of New York. By 1850, successful communities in the Bronx, Brooklyn, and Manhattan included Sacred Heart Sisters (1841), the Sisters of Mercy (1846), Dominican Sisters (1853), Ursuline Sisters (1855), Good Shepherd Sisters (1855), and Sisters of Saint Joseph (1856).[3]

These women were taking part in a transatlantic revitalization of the religious life for women in the Catholic Church, as new communities were organized and memberships in new and old soared. A relatively new kind of sisterhood—what was to come to be called an active community—was especially popular. First organized in the late 17th century in spite of Church law that required enclosure for nuns, it proved to be an extremely attractive life choice for Catholic women in 19th and 20th century Europe and the United States as they looked for a religious life that, through ministry, addressed social problems of the day.[4]

Sisters who settled in New York did so on their own initiative and through the efforts of the hierarchy, individual clergy, and laypeople. Bishop John Hughes, who presided over the New York diocese and archdiocese from 1842 to 1864, personally brought the Irish Sisters of Mercy from London to New York, where Elizabeth Seton's daughter became their first postulant. Reverend Stephen Raffeiner, pastor of Most Holy Trinity church in Williamsburg and vicar general, was influential in bringing the Dominican Sisters there. (They had come from Germany intending to settle elsewhere.) The foundation of the Sisters of St. Joseph in Brooklyn was financed by Rosine Parmentier, daughter and sister of two other prominent female Catholic benefactors.

2
Hoffmann's Catholic Directory, Almanac and Clergy List-Quarterly 1886, 1887 (Milwaukee and Chicago: Hoffmann Bros., 1886, 1887), *1896* (Milwaukee: Hoffman Brothers, 1896), and *1899* (Milwaukee: M. H. Wiltzius).
3
Hoffmann's Catholic Directory 1886, 91; Sister Ursula Clarke, O.S.U., *The Ursulines in Cork* (Blackrock, Cork: Ursuline Convent, 1996), 52–54; Reverend Monsignor Florence D. Cohalan, *A Popular History of the Archdiocese of New York* (Yonkers: U.S. Historical Society, 1983), 58; Mary Ewens, *The Role of the Nun in Nineteenth Century America* (New York: Arno Press, 1978), 63–74, 148ff.; Evangeline Thomas, C.S.J., *Women Religious History Sources* (New York: R. R. Bowker, 1983), 80, 89–90.
4
Ewens, *Role of the Nun*, 63–74.

LEFT

Lois Hobart Black, [Religious of the Holy Union of the Sacred Hearts watching parade from convent, 15 East 96th Street, Manhattan], c. 1950, gelatin silver print
The Religious of the Holy Union of the Sacred Hearts taught at the school of St. Francis de Sales parish on East 97th Street. Their convent at 15 East 96th Street had been designed by architect Ogden Codman, Jr., in 1915–1916 for his client Lucy D. Dahlgren.

TOP

A.D. Fisk, *Sister Irene [Fitzgibbon] and Her Flock,* c. 1890, from one of two halves of a stereo dry plate negative
Sister Mary Irene Fitzgibbon (1823–1896), a Sister of Charity, founded the New York Foundling Hospital, seen here, in 1869.

NEW YORK FOUNDLING HOSPITAL.

TOP

Byron Co, [Engraving of New York Foundling Hospital], c. 1882

The Foundling's East 68th Street campus, begun in 1873, expanded to include St. Ann's Maternity Hospital in 1880. St. John's Pediatric Hospital opened in February 1882, completing facilities dedicated to the care of children in need.

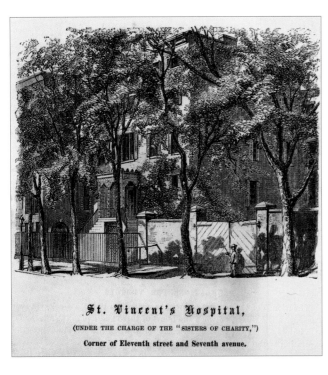

St. Vincent's Hospital,

(UNDER THE CHARGE OF THE "SISTERS OF CHARITY,")

Corner of Eleventh street and Seventh avenue.

Roman Catholic Orphan Asylum.

BOTTOM LEFT

St. Vincent's Hospital, c. 1870, engraving

St. Vincent's Hospital opened in November 1849 under the auspices of the Sisters of Charity, as the first Catholic hospital in greater New York. New York bishop John Hughes's sister Ellen, known as Sister Angela Hughes within her community, was one of the sisters assigned to the hospital.

BOTTOM RIGHT

Roman Catholic Orphan Asylum, c. 1870, engraving

Caring for both boys and girls lodged at the Roman Catholic Orphan Asylum prompted the establishment of a separate congregation of the Sisters of Charity within the New York Archdiocese in the mid 1840s. The Maryland-based order's rule had precluded teaching or working with boys.

Notably, the Sisters of St. Joseph, a French community, were first invited to the United States because their community was flexible about their work—they did not have a prohibition about teaching boys, which some other French communities had. Their rule, the guide sisterhoods follow in the organization of their lives, was such that it could adapt to American conditions, as it certainly did in Brooklyn and Queens, where the community flourished.[5]

Sisterhoods carefully cultivated close relationships with the Catholic laity of all classes, and those relationships facilitated their work. Sisters wisely chose their board members and cultivated Ladies Aid Associations, which were often filled with former students, thus creating networks of supporters. Financial contributions came from the powerful as well as from the less so. Some communities literally took to the streets, soliciting contributions, planting members outside factories, on the docks, and at the racetrack, where they knew Catholics would find it hard to turn down sisters' requests. The annual reports of their institutions carefully noted contributions large and small and suggest that a public affiliation with their work was important to many Catholics.[6]

By the outbreak of the Civil War, sisters were very much a part of the Church's efforts to maintain the faith of immigrant New Yorkers, so much so that Bishop Hughes was initially reluctant to let any sisters answer the War Department's request for their services. But Sisters of Mercy did go to the battlefield with other New Yorkers, and Sisters of Charity nursed soldiers in the city, running a military hospital for the War Department at their former motherhouse at McGowan's Pass in Central Park. As Mary Denis Mahr has suggested, the sisters' war work, carried out despite opposition from nativists, went a long way toward improving attitudes about sisters among some Americans. Earlier images of sinister convent life depicted in the best-selling tale of escaped nun Maria Monk—*Awful Disclosures of the Hotel Dieu Nunnery*, first published in 1836—were supplanted by ones of benevolent nursing nuns.[7]

New York sisterhoods, like the immigrants they served, were what is now referred to as "ethnic." New York foundations, often of European origins, began with specific national identities and cultural practices, particularly language in the case of German communities. Shared identities, origins, and work within one specific group remained strong well into the 20th century among some groups, such as the Felician Sisters, who served Polish Catholics in Brooklyn, and the Franciscan Handmaids of Mary, who came to New York in 1923 to work among African Americans in Harlem. Communities with European origins experienced, as did the immigrants they served, an Americanization process in the move overseas. As Patricia Byrne has illustrated, the Sisters of St. Joseph in Brooklyn, like all the community's foundations in the United States, were independent and separate from the motherhouse in France, but issues of language and custom created tensions even as the community flourished in an American environment. Mother Frances Xavier Cabrini (1850–1917) brought the

5

Patricia Byrne, C.S.J., "Sisters of St. Joseph: The Americanization of a French Tradition," *U.S. Catholic Historian* 5 (summer/fall 1986): 254; Reverend E. J. Crawford, *The Daughters of Dominic on Long Island* (New York: Benziger Brothers, 1938), 26–28, 49–51; Margaret Quinn, C.S.J., "Sylvia, Adele and Rosine Parmentier: 19th Century Women of Brooklyn," *U.S. Catholic Historian* 5 (summer/fall 1986): 350–351; George C. Stewart Jr., *Marvels of Charity* (Huntington, Ind.: Our Sunday Visitor, 1994), 25.

6

Bernadette McCauley, *Who Shall Take Care of Our Sick? Roman Catholic Sisters and the Development of Catholic Hospitals in New York City* (Baltimore: Johns Hopkins University Press, 2005), 54–58.

7

Ewens, *Role of the Nun*, 18–21; Sister Mary Denis Maher, *To Bind Up the Wounds: Catholic Sister Nurses in the U.S. Civil War* (Baton Rouge: Louisiana State University Press, 1999), 73–74, 80, 156–159.

TOP

Barat Day Nursery, after 1915
Barat Settlement on Chrystie Street, run by alumnae of the New York City schools sponsored by the Religious of the Sacred Heart of Jesus and sodalists of the Children of Mary, provided a nursery for working mothers beginning in 1915.

BOTTOM

Classroom at the Madison Avenue school of the Convent of the Sacred Heart, 1929
Religious orders operated schools and academies independent of the Archdiocesan parochial school system.

FACING PAGE

Joseph Schwartz, *Nun on the "A" Train,* 1940s

Missionary Sisters of the Sacred Heart from Italy to New York for the care of Italian immigrants in 1889, but while that continued to be the mission of the community, not all sisters were of Italian origin. In her study of Cabrini's early efforts to recruit postulants, Mary Louise Sullivan found that Cabrini's first two New York postulants were Irish. They were sent to Italy for novitiate training, but soon after that an American novitiate made that unnecessary, and American Irish women continued to join the community, along with women from other European backgrounds.[8]

Sisterhoods looked to maintain specific identities—such as traditions within a group and very powerful identification with their own foundress and her mission—but there were strong similarities in their work. Many people tend to associate sisters most closely with parochial-school education, but in the 19th and early 20th centuries, other institutional work in health care and social welfare was very strong, and within that, there was an emphasis on the particular circumstances of women and children. As Maureen Fitzgerald has shown, New York sisters created a unique Catholic form of child-welfare service, which looked to help families through hard times by temporarily housing children, always with the ultimate goal of family unification. Catholic child care was a revolving door of care: Sisters provided refuge in difficult times. The need for help of this kind was staggering. The largest of sister orphanages in the city, the New York Foundling Home on Manhattan's East Side, described by historians Dorothy Brown and Elizabeth McKeown as "imposing," housed 2,700 infants in 1895.[9]

In so much of their work, sisters provided models that were replicated by others. In their early hospitals, they offered care—again, a refuge of sorts—at a time when many New Yorkers, with good reason, feared hospitals. The earliest sisters' hospitals were smaller than the massive charity hospitals run by the municipal authorities and, moreover, did not include the Protestant evangelizing that Catholic patients routinely received as patients in other hospitals, including public ones. While hospital sisters certainly prayed for their patients, their efforts also included careful nursing and up-to-date therapeutics. And in doing so, as in the case of their Civil War nursing, they often received the grudging praise of New Yorkers not predisposed to a favorable view of Catholics or Catholicism.[10]

For New York Catholics, associations with particular sisterhoods remain strong among those who at one time or another found themselves under the care of sisters. In some cases, the connection is a very personal one: former vice presidential candidate Geraldine Ferraro of Queens, for example, has recalled how a Sister of the Sacred Heart was her "navigator" at their secondary school at Marymount. In others, a particular sisterhood was a tremendous presence during formative years, reaching within and across generations. Again, numbers are useful indicators: Ferraro's navigator was one of several thousand sisters teaching in postwar New York.[11]

8
Byrne, "Sisters of St. Joseph": 241-272; Mary Louise Sullivan, M.S.C., *Mother Cabrini* (New York: Center for Migration Studies, 1992), 104–105.

9
Dorothy M. Brown and Elizabeth McKeown, *The Poor Belong to Us* (Cambridge, Mass.: Harvard University Press, 1997), 87, 90; Maureen Fitzgerald, *Habits of Compassion* (Urbana: University of Illinois Press, 2006).

10
McCauley, *Who Shall Take Care of Our Sick?*, 5–7, 25, 134–136.

11
Geraldine A. Ferraro, *Framing a Life* (New York: Scribner), 66; *The Official Catholic Directory* (New York: P. J. Kenedy, 1950), 2.

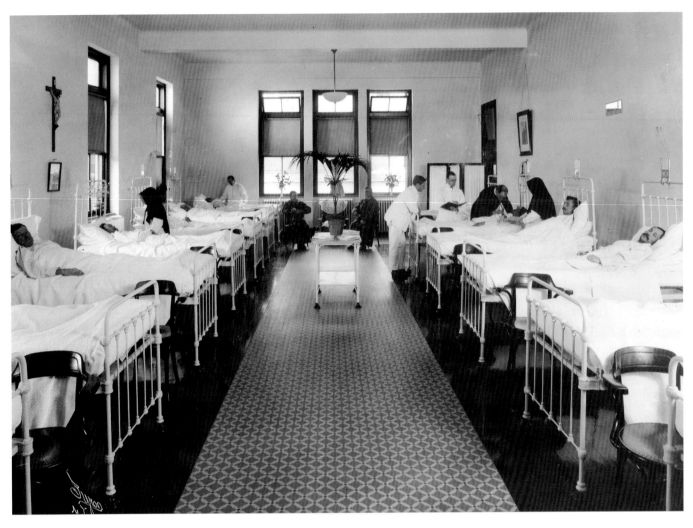

TOP
View of men's ward, St. Francis Hospital,
Brook Avenue & E. 142nd St., Bronx,
c. 1910, gelatin silver print
In 1910, 36 Sisters of the Poor of St. Francis
staffed the Bronx hospital.

BOTTOM
Mabel Dwight (1875–1955), *Silence*,
1935–40, lithograph

Images of sisters remain strong in popular culture even though fewer wear the kind of clothing that made them so identifiable in the Glackens picture, so much so that sociologist Mark Massa has suggested sisters are "the most likely icon of things Catholic."[12] But their importance to the history of Catholicism in New York is far more than representational. Sisters have unique lives: being of the city, entrenched in their work, but apart from it, too, within the religious life of a sisterhood. For many of them, it is an empowering life. For many New York Catholics, sisters brought the church into their lives in a very personal way.

[12]
Mark S. Massa, *Catholics and American Culture: Fulton Sheen, Dorothy Day, and the Notre Dame Football Team* (New York: Crossroad, 1999), 175.

Nuns learning artificial respiration, 1954
Nuns from 12 Roman Catholic religious
communities practiced artificial respiration on pupils at St. Agnes Parochial
School as part of a course to qualify
them as Red Cross First Aid Instructors
in Archdiocesan parochial schools.

JAMES THOMAS KEANE

BRIDGING THE RACIAL GAP

JOHN LAFARGE AND THE CATHOLIC INTERRACIAL COUNCIL

In the world of 20th-century racial politics, the name of Father John LaFarge, S.J., loomed large for many decades. This famous New York Jesuit wore any number of hats during his long career, many of them simultaneously: priest, journalist, editor, lecturer, community organizer, interracial pioneer, ecumenicist, and pundit on matters ranging from aesthetics to atheism to the vagaries of old age. But any commentator on his life would point to his efforts and achievements in race relations as the defining work of his career.

LaFarge was born in 1880 in Newport, Rhode Island, into an aristocratic and artistic family. His mother was a descendant of Benjamin Franklin, and his father, also named John, was a famous artist and a close friend of novelist Henry James and Isaac Hecker (founder of the Paulists) and was renowned not only for his paintings but also for his extraordinary work with stained glass. One of the elder LaFarge's sons was a well-known architect, and his grandsons Christopher and Oliver LaFarge became prominent writers, the latter also a famous anthropologist and winner of a 1929 Pulitzer Prize for his novel *Laughing Boy*.

The younger John LaFarge graduated from Harvard in 1901, leaving shortly after for Innsbruck, Austria, to begin study for the priesthood. In his autobiography, *The Manner Is Ordinary*, LaFarge recounts with irony a conversation he shared with his mother (a convert to Catholicism) upon his departure: "For some reason or other, which neither she nor I could ever explain, she begged me on that occasion: 'Don't let them make you a Jesuit.' I replied, 'Mother, dear, nothing can ever make me a Jesuit.'"[1] He was wrong. Less than four years lat-

[1] LaFarge, John, S.J., *The Manner Is Ordinary* (New York: Harcourt Brace, 1954), 76-77.

109

er, LaFarge found himself in Rome, seeking permission to enter the Jesuits, citing as a primary reason his profound wish to know the material poverty of Jesus. "The idea of being a priest and of not sharing the poverty of the great High Priest seemed to me intolerable," LaFarge later wrote.[2] He was ordained in July 1905 and entered the Jesuit novitiate of the New York-Maryland Province in November of that same year.

After several years of academic training and short-term assignments, LaFarge was sent in 1911 to St. Mary's County in southern Maryland, a rural area with a mixed racial population, where the Jesuits first established mission churches in 1663. Through his work in the mission churches, LaFarge saw firsthand the burdens and scars inflicted on the area's impoverished African Americans. The experience affected LaFarge deeply and set him on the path he would follow in various ways for the rest of his life, working on behalf of African Americans both within the Church and in the country at large.

More so than any individual project, his persistent and eloquent defenses of desegregation, interracial dialogue, and a greater sensitivity to the plight of African Americans began in those years and earned him a reputation as a giant in the area of race relations. In 1924, he founded the Cardinal Gibbons Institute, a project which began as an industrial school for African-American young men. Despite "a disheartening obstacle of general public indifference to anything connected with the South or the Negro," LaFarge claimed "tremendous interest in the whole idea of a project that was national in scope, the first national project undertaken by Catholics on behalf of the Negro."[3] In truth, the school never outlived its early growing pains, hurt both by indifference and by the national financial catastrophe of 1929. However, the leaders whom LaFarge met and cultivated in that endeavor would prove invaluable in future projects.

In 1926, LaFarge was appointed to the staff of *America*, the national Catholic journal of politics, religion, and the arts published by Jesuits and based in Manhattan. The assignment radically changed the scope and nature of his work for the remaining 37 years of his life, as he moved ever more prominently into the world of writing and public speaking. While he did not entirely leave behind his previous interests—he retained close ties to the Catholic Rural Life Movement and was in constant touch with his many colleagues from his Maryland days—his work at *America* introduced him to a new world.

In New York, LaFarge encountered a racial dynamic very different from his Maryland experience. There, Catholic whites and African Americans had coexisted, however awkwardly, for centuries in a largely rural setting. In New York, African Americans made up barely two percent of the Catholic population and were widely resented by lower-income white ethnic groups with whom they competed for work. Furthermore, when white Catholics in New York and other northern cities talked about "race" in the decades before World War II, they

2
Ibid, 119.

3
LaFarge, *The Manner Is Ordinary*, 212, 213.

Father LaFarge with children from St. Mary's parish, Maryland, c. 1924

BOTTOM
John LaFarge before his ordination, 1901
This photograph was taken upon LaFarge's graduation from Harvard University.

NEXT SPREAD
Father LaFarge with students from St. Peter Claver School in Maryland, 1939

often were referring to themselves and their different language and ethnic traditions. The hatred of many white Catholics for African Americans existed across ethnic lines, often rivaling or even exceeding the racial tensions of the South. Perhaps a classic case of displaced abjection, the psychological process by which marginalized groups turned their discontent and aggression against even more disadvantaged groups rather than upon those in authority, had been playing out in New York at least since the draft riots of 1863.[4]

LaFarge began writing on issues of interracial dialogue and racism almost immediately after arriving at the magazine, and he immersed himself in the academic study of the race question. In 1934, he founded the Catholic Interracial Council of New York, a group whose structure and aims were duplicated by similar endeavors around the nation. Based on his Cardinal Gibbons Institute as well as the Catholic Laymen's Union in New York, the Catholic Interracial Council included among its goals the elimination of ignorance regarding race issues, social justice on the model of the old Catholic Action movement, and a struggle against communism. By 1960, there were 42 Catholic Interracial Councils around the United States, and they had joined together as the National Catholic Conference on Interracial Justice in 1958. In later years, Catholic Interracial Councils gained popularity with political activists as a way to improve dialogue among racial groups, and in their heyday in the 1960s they were popular with college students.

In 1937, America Press published LaFarge's most important book on race relations, *Interracial Justice: A Study of the Catholic Doctrine of Race Relations*, which grew out of his philosophical education as well as his experiences in Maryland and New York in the 1920s and 1930s. The book laid out a lengthy argument for rethinking American racial attitudes, particularly racist attitudes toward the perceived lack of African-American intellectual or economic achievements, which LaFarge attributed to economic and cultural impoverishment. Using his training in philosophical Thomism, he argued that human rights were natural to all people regardless of race, class, or creed. In this sense, the rights of individual Americans were not bestowed by the U.S. Constitution, but were merely asserted by it. The Constitution "is not the source of origin of our natural rights," LaFarge argued. "It is the governmental instrument by which the national sovereignty guarantees...those natural rights which the citizen enjoys by virtue of the very fact that he is a citizen and as such is vested with certain rights as he is bound by certain duties."[5]

This argument impressed an unlikely reader, Pope Pius XI, who in 1938 asked LaFarge to help write an encyclical on racism; Pius had been impressed by the portability of LaFarge's natural law argument, which could be applied to any society's racist policies, including those of Nazi Germany. The encyclical was never released; in fact, it took years before its existence and LaFarge's participation were revealed.[6]

4
McGreevy, John T., *Parish Boundaries: The Catholic Encounter with Race in the Twentieth-Century Urban North* (Chicago: University of Chicago Press, 1996), 7, 29–39.
5
LaFarge, John, S.J., *Interracial Justice* (New York: America Press, 1937), 61.
6
Hecht, Robert A., *An Unordinary Man: A Life of Father John LaFarge, S.J.* (Lanham: Scarecrow Press, 1996), 103.

Despite his opposition to interracial marriage (because of the social damage he believed it would cause children), LaFarge made a strong case for the immorality of American segregation on practical grounds, saying that when mandated by law, segregation "imputes essential inferiority to the segregated group" and actually would end up hurting the groups enforcing it by depriving them of the cultural and economic benefits of free exchange. This approach exemplified LaFarge's ability to combine philosophical and religious reasoning with practical, politically sensible approaches to social ills. He reworked the text and added four more chapters for the 1943 release of *The Race Question and the Negro*.[7]

LaFarge became executive editor of *America* in 1942 and then editor-in-chief between 1944 and 1948, establishing during his tenure the progressive editorial tilt that the magazine retains to this day. He continued to write extensively on race relations, but also contributed his thoughts regularly on labor, foreign affairs, McCarthyism, Catholic liturgical debates, and countless other issues. He continued his prominent involvement in the burgeoning Civil Rights movement throughout the 1950s, but his influence declined as the movement benefited from the emergence of African-American leaders and took on a more aggressive tone at odds with LaFarge's more conciliatory approach.

Increasingly frail as he moved into his 80s, LaFarge continued to work at *America* until he died on November 24, 1963, two days after the assassination of President John F. Kennedy. Only three months earlier, LaFarge had been present on the speaker's platform for Martin Luther King, Jr.'s famous "I Have a Dream" speech. Upon the news of LaFarge's death, Cardinal Cushing of Boston, who was in Washington, D.C., for the president's funeral, immediately flew to New York to celebrate the funeral mass at St. Ignatius Loyola church on the Upper East Side, an event that drew hundreds of mourners, including almost every prominent civil rights leader in the nation. Cushing spoke at length of the "three Johns" the world dearly needed and yet had recently lost: Kennedy, LaFarge, and Pope John XXIII.[8]

"He was never one to identify the status quo with the Law of God," commented *America's* editors in an editorial shortly after, "nor, by the same token, to lose the vision of ultimate and abiding values underlying social change."[9] A year later, *America* editor-in-chief Thurston N. Davis, S.J., spoke of LaFarge's overwhelming importance for the development of the magazine while announcing the creation of an institute bearing LaFarge's name: "Whatever influence [*America* has] today, what authority we can muster in the world of the press, we owe largely to this gently dogged priest whose broad sympathy for his fellow man spanned the whole world round and constantly spilled over onto our pages."[10]

LaFarge was not without his detractors, both among his peers during his lifetime and among historians today. Recent biographers have pointed out that for all his progressive ideas on race, LaFarge could also be blind to his own paternalistic tendencies and those

7

LaFarge, John, S.J., *The Race Question and the Negro* (New York: Longmans Green, 1943), 152–59.

8

Hecht, *An Unordinary Man*, 252–54.

9

Davis, Thurston, S.J. "John LaFarge, S.J. (1880-1963)," *America Magazine*, December 7, 1963.

10

Davis, Thurston, S.J. "Announcing the John LaFarge Institute in the New America House," *America Magazine*, June 6, 1964.

of other white pioneers for racial justice, particularly when it came to appointing African Americans to positions of authority or recognizing the urgency of their situation. LaFarge was also capable of allowing his fear of communism to color his ideas on race and class, to the extent that he sometimes promoted interracial activities as a way of counteracting Communist infiltration into American minority politics. These tendencies hurt LaFarge's influence in the Civil Rights movement in the crucial years of the late 1950s and early 1960s, particularly as he had already reached a ripe old age before the movement gained real momentum. These are minor blemishes on a distinguished career, but ones for which his peers and his later critics rightly took him to task.

No better summation of LaFarge's life exists than his own formulation at the conclusion of his autobiography, when this famous man of social action and letters issued the following challenge: "Nothing will convert the world short of a gospel of limitless love; nothing short of a gospel of scrupulous faithfulness to the rights of the humblest person and to our pledges with man and God. I know no finer test of a man's sincerity than his willingness to work constructively for the world reign of love, justice, and law."[11]

11
LaFarge, *The Manner Is Ordinary*, 378.

TOP

Members of the New York Catholic Interracial Council, Chicago, 1958

In 1934, Father LaFarge founded the first CIC in New York. Two decades later, there were 42 such councils across the country and, in 1958, they convened in Chicago for the first National Catholic Conference on Interracial Justice.

BOTTOM LEFT

Father LaFarge with members of the Catholic Interracial Council, undated

BOTTOM RIGHT

Father LaFarge, c. 1959

PUBLISHED BY J. SEINER.

Corner Stone Laid August 15th 1858.
by his Eminence
John, Archbishop Hughes.

THE NEW CATHEDRAL.

To be completed by his Eminence
John Cardinal McCloskey
First Cardinal of America

SANCTIFIED LIVES

Among the millions of Catholics who have called New York home since the founding of the New York and Brooklyn dioceses, five have been singled out for their exemplary lives, their piety, and their devotion to their faith. Elizabeth Ann Bayley Seton became the first American-born saint in 1975, while Frances Xavier Cabrini, an Italian immigrant, was the first U.S. citizen to be canonized when she was declared a saint in 1946. Three other New Yorkers are under consideration for sainthood: Pierre Toussaint, Isaac Thomas Hecker, and Dorothy Day. Their lives speak to the diversity of experience—and the unity of faith—in Catholic New York.

PIERRE TOUSSAINT

Of the many immigrant Catholics who settled in New York City in the 18th century, Pierre Toussaint surely was among the most extraordinary. He was born into slavery in present-day Haiti in 1766 and was brought to New York in 1787, when his owner fled the French colony, only to die within a year of resettling in the city. Toussaint assisted his owner's widow, now destitute, and in gratitude she freed him before she died in 1807.

Even when he was in bondage, Toussaint was a regular worshipper at Saint Peter's church in downtown Manhattan. Once free, he became a highly successful hairdresser for the city's wealthy merchant class. Toussaint and his wife, Juliette, used a portion of their earnings to support St. Peter's—the church in which they were married—St. Vincent de Paul church, and the Catholic Orphan Asylum. They had no children of their own, but they brought into their homes children of African descent struggling against injustice and discrimination. The children, whose parents were either dead or unable to care for their offspring, remained with the Toussaints until they were able to support themselves.

Although Pierre Toussaint became a beloved figure in New York's Catholic community, he suffered from the injustices that were heaped upon men and women of African descent in antebellum New York. Once, while he was worshipping in old Saint Patrick's Cathedral on Mulberry Street, an usher loudly objected to his presence in the congregation.

TOP
Anthony Meucci, *Pierre Toussaint*, c. 1825
watercolor on ivory

LEFT
The New Cathedral [Saint Patrick's
Cathedral], undated, colored lithograph
published by John Stiner

Toussaint died in 1853 and was buried in the cemetery of old St. Patrick's. In the mid-1990s, Cardinal John O'Connor requested that Toussaint's remains be moved from the cemetery to a crypt in the current St. Patrick's Cathedral. At around the same time, Toussaint was declared "Venerable," the first step in the canonization process.

—*Terry Golway*

ELIZABETH ANN BAYLEY SETON

Elizabeth Ann Bayley was born in New York in August 1774 into an Episcopal family that was among the area's earliest colonial settlers. At the time of Elizabeth's birth, the Setons were well established and financially secure.

She was the daughter of Dr. Richard Bayley and Catherine Charlton, who died when Elizabeth was just three years old. She was a voracious reader, displaying an intellectual curiosity that would influence her theological search later on.

In 1794, at age 19, Elizabeth married William Magee Seton, a prosperous New York merchant, and by 1802, the couple had five children: Anna Maria (b. 1795), William (b. 1796), Richard (b. 1798), Catherine (b. 1800), and Rebecca (b. 1802). Elizabeth managed to find time to co-found, along with Isabella Marshall Graham, the Society for the Relief of Poor Widows with Small Children in 1797.

Not long after the Setons' fifth child was born, their prosperous world collapsed. Their businesses declined dramatically, and finally they were forced to declare bankruptcy. At around the same time, 1803, William Seton developed tuberculosis, and he died while he and Elizabeth were in Italy in a vain attempt to find a cure.

While waiting to bring her husband's body home, Elizabeth was introduced to Catholicism by several friends. She decided to convert after returning home, and on Ash Wednesday, March 14, 1805, Elizabeth Seton was received into the Catholic Church by Father Matthew O'Brien in St. Peter's Church on Barclay Street.

At the urging of Father William DuBourg, president of St. Mary's Seminary, Elizabeth went to Baltimore in 1808 to set up a school for girls. The following year, she moved her school to Emmitsburg, Maryland. It was there that she founded a new community: the Sisters of Charity of Saint Joseph. On July 19, 1813, 18 sisters, including Elizabeth Seton, made vows of poverty, chastity, obedience, and service to the poor. The community elected Elizabeth as their first superior and would continue to re-elect her until her death.

Mother Seton's community founded and ran orphanages, asylums, hospitals, and schools to support Catholic communities throughout the fledgling republic. She died in 1821, at the

Pierre Toussaint, undated

MIDDLE
C. B. J. F. de Saint-Memin (1770–1821), *Elizabeth Ann Bayley Seton [Mrs. William Seton]*, 1797, engraving

BOTTOM
Mother Elizabeth Seton, photographed 1931

age of 46, near Emmitsburg. She was beatified in 1963 and canonized by Pope Paul VI in 1975, the first American-born saint. —*Catherine Nicholson*

ISAAC THOMAS HECKER

New York native Isaac Thomas Hecker's personal spiritual quest took him from a Manhattan bakery to Rome, where in 1858 he received papal authorization to found the first male religious community organized within the Archdiocese of New York, the Congregation of Missionary Priests of St. Paul the Apostle (better known as the Paulist Fathers).

Born into a working-class German immigrant family in New York City in 1819, Hecker attended Methodist services in his youth. While his brothers expanded the family bakery and milling businesses, Hecker pursued a course of spiritual development documented by biographer David J. O'Brien in his 1992 study, *Isaac Hecker: An American Catholic*. With financial assistance from his older brother, George, he traveled from the New England transcendentalism of the utopian communities Brook Farm and Fruitlands to the Catholic Church and then to the Roman Catholic priesthood. Baptized by Bishop John McCloskey in late June 1844, Hecker traveled to a novitiate of the German Redemptorist order in Belgium the following year and was ordained in October 1849. Hecker returned to New York City on March 19, 1851, as one of a band of Redemptorist priests who traveled the country, presenting English-language missions to American Catholics.

Hecker became a noted preacher, lecturer, and writer who appealed not only to Catholics but also to mixed, Protestant, or unchurched audiences. His publications, beginning with *Questions of the Soul* (1855), made him known outside the Catholic community.

After the Vatican refused to allow Hecker and four colleagues to establish an English-speaking Redemptorist house, the five clerics were released from their Redemptorist vows and authorized to begin a new missionary community.

TOP
Father Isaac Hecker, 1878, engraving, from John Gilmary Shea, editor, *The Catholic Churches of New York City* (New York: Lawrence G. Goulding & Co., 1878)

BOTTOM
The Church of St. Paul the Apostle, c. 1878, from John Gilmary Shea, editor, *The Catholic Churches of New York City* (New York: Lawrence G. Goulding & Co., 1878)

Under an agreement in July 1858 with John Hughes, archbishop of New York, the new community was given responsibility for a parish initially extending from West 52nd Street to 109th Street on Manhattan's West Side. The Paulists solicited funds for a parish church and community house, with the largest donation coming from George Hecker. The Paulist Fathers acquired land at 59th Street, west of Ninth Avenue, which remains the parish center. The current church building opened in 1885. Hecker was the first pastor of St. Paul's as well as the first superior-general of the Paulists. The Church of St. Paul the Apostle became a model modern parish under the leadership of Hecker and his successors.

Hecker also founded the first Catholic national monthly literary magazine, *The Catholic World* (1865), the monthly *Young Catholic* (1870), and *The Catholic Publication Society* (1866), which

121

evolved into the *Columbus Press* (1891), and then the *Paulist Press* (1916), to print and distribute popular religious pamphlets explaining Catholic doctrine and encouraging devotional life. Hecker died at age 69 in December 1888. His cause for sainthood was opened recently.
—*Deborah Dependahl Waters*

ST. FRANCES XAVIER CABRINI

St. Frances Xavier Cabrini was born in Lombardy, Italy, in July 1850, one of 13 children, only four of whom survived to adulthood. At 13, Mother Cabrini went to study with the Daughters of the Sacred Heart, and though she was certified as a teacher at 18, she later contracted smallpox and so was refused admission to the order. Disappointed, she returned to teach in a school in Sant'Angelo founded by her sister, Rosa. In 1874, she was asked by diocesan authorities to take over an orphanage in Codogno, a nearby town. There, in 1877, she entered the religious life, adding Xavier to her name in a tribute to the Spanish Jesuit missionary Francis Xavier. Like Xavier, Mother Cabrini hoped to bring the Gospel to China.

In 1880, she founded a new congregation, the Missionary Sisters of the Sacred Heart of Jesus, which she hoped would be instrumental in establishing schools and orphanages worldwide. By 1885, the Missionary Sisters had founded seven homes and a school, all of which brought Mother Cabrini to the attention of Bishop Scalabrini, founder of the Missionary Institute of St. Charles Borremeo, and the Pope, Leo XIII.

Pope Leo was worried about the lack of help for Italian Catholics in the United States who were under increased pressure to join various Protestant denominations that were organizing in urban areas. Both Scalabrini and Leo thought Cabrini and her order would be ideal to help give support to the immigrant Italian women. Mother Cabrini and six Missionary Sisters arrived in New York in March 1889.

The sisters' first night brought them into the all too real and harsh immigrant world as they spent the night in a tenement in the Italian section of the Lower East Side. After meeting with the archbishop of New York, Michael Corrigan, Cabrini won permission to set up an orphanage in West Park, in Ulster County, New York, which was to be the first of 67 orphanages, hospitals, nurseries, and schools she founded.

Two particular projects established by Mother Cabrini deserve special attention: the establishment of bilingual schools in Italian and English, and the foundation of a trade school for women next to Our Lady of Pompeii Church on Carmine Street in Manhattan.

Mother Cabrini followed the route of many immigrants when she became a naturalized citizen in 1909, and she continued her work until she died in 1917 of complications from malaria in Chicago. Her body is now enshrined in Hudson Heights, New York. She was

TOP
Gonippo Raggi, mural depicting St. Frances Xavier Cabrini (1850–1917) as patron saint of immigrants, undated

BOTTOM
Children praying at the St. Frances Xavier Cabrini shrine maintained by the Missionary Sisters of the Sacred Heart of Jesus, Hudson Heights, 1946

beatified in 1938 by Pope Pius XI, and in 1946 she became the first U.S. citizen to be canonized. She is, fittingly, the patron saint of immigrants. —*Catherine Nicholson*

DOROTHY DAY

Dorothy Day is one of the best-known Catholic women in America. Her passion for social justice, her defense of the poor and homeless, her insistence on nonviolence, and her co-founding with Peter Maurin of the Catholic Worker Movement, challenged the values of American society in the 20th century.

Day was born into an Episcopal family in Brooklyn in 1897. She attended the University of Illinois from 1914 to 1917, but dropped out and moved back to New York City, where she worked as reporter for *The Call* and later *The Masses*, two of the more radical papers of the time. She was arrested in 1917 for her part in a women's suffrage protest outside the White House.

In 1924, she bought a small cottage on Staten Island and began a relationship with Forster Batterham, an anarchist and biologist. In 1927, they had a daughter, Tamar Theresa. Day had begun attending a local Catholic church and wished to have the child baptized, but Batterham opposed the idea. He left Day when she went ahead with the baptism. She then took her spiritual journey even further when, on December 28, 1927, she was received into the Catholic Church at Our Lady Help of Christians church in the Tottenville section of Staten Island.

In 1932, Day met Peter Maurin, who wanted Day to publish a journal espousing Catholic social teaching and encouraging peaceful, nonviolent ways to end poverty, hunger, and homelessness. Thus began *The Catholic Worker*, which is still published today.

The Catholic Worker Movement soon spread into a national organization with 33 homes for the unemployed and otherwise homeless. The movement preached pacifism, a position that became unpopular after the Japanese bombed Pearl Harbor and the United States entered World War II. Nevertheless, Day remained resolute, insisting that all issues could be solved peacefully. Her position caused a split in the Worker movement, forcing the closure of about half the organization's homes for the poor.

Day's work after the war involved a mixture of protest: against nuclear weapons, for which she was jailed on a number of occasions; for civil rights, which resulted in the Ku Klux Klan bombing one of the Workers' homes; and for world peace, for which she fasted and prayed.

Day died in 1980, insisting she was not a saint, just someone not embarrassed to talk about God. In 1983, the Claretian Missionaries proposed her for sainthood, and in 2000, Pope John Paul II granted the Archdiocese of New York permission to open Day's cause, calling her a "Servant of God," the first step in the canonization process. —*Catherine Nicholson*

TOP
Dorothy Day (1897–1980), 1916

BOTTOM
Catholic Worker staff, New York, 1930s

[The sachems of Tammany Hall], 1929
Museum of the City of New York,
gift of The Family of Governor Alfred E. Smith,
45.117.260

PUBLIC FACES: CATHOLICS IN LABOR AND POLITICS

Peter A. Quinn (standing) speaking at the
dedication of the new St. Raymond's School
on Purdy Street, the Bronx, c. 1951

Life of the Party

He concedes that a morally pure society, with candidates unblemished with sin and vice, might exist somewhere, though he has never seen or heard of one, and can't really imagine what one would be like. "But I'll keep looking," he concludes.
—WILLIAM KENNEDY, ROSCOE

Peter A. Quinn, my father, was a most imperfect man. Moody, often emotionally distant, capable of purple-faced tantrums that seemed certain—although they never did—to end in his death or the death of anyone in the near vicinity, he was also a good man. The older I get, the longer I've been around high-ranking politicians and corporate executives, the more I've realized his goodness. He was uninterested in wealth and power. He was devoid of pomposity and self-importance. A judge for 25 years in city and state courts, he approached his job with an equal sense of responsibility and humility. He was capable of laughing at himself and had a gut-seated sympathy for the poor, the powerless, and the disenfranchised.

Several times, learning that my father had spent his life in politics—Bronx politics, no less—strangers have responded jocularly, "You must be rich!" I've laughed along with them. My father died in 1974 with accumulated life savings of $16,000. At the same time, amid the hours I've spent reading about Tammany Hall and New York's rampant political skullduggery, I wondered about my father's experiences in Bronx politics as an assemblyman, congressman, and judge, about the corruption he undoubtedly knew of and, perhaps, closed his eyes to.

When my father entered politics in the early 1930s, the leader (newspapers invariably referred to him as "boss") of the Bronx Democratic Organization was Ed Flynn. An intimate of Franklin Delano Roosevelt,

Flynn ran a relatively "clean machine." It wasn't devoid, by any means, of the self-dealing and "honest graft" described long before by George Washington Plunkitt; but especially in comparison to Prendergast's machine in Kansas City or Hague's in Jersey City—or even the Tammany machine in Manhattan—it was free of an avaricious disregard for legality.

My father's political initiation came during the investigations of Judge Samuel Seabury into the multiple layers of graft, bribery, and venal shenanigans piled atop one another in the administration of Mayor Jimmy Walker. When bosses in other boroughs ordered their followers in the state assembly to vote against the continuation of the Joint Legislative Committee investigating the government of New York City, Flynn stood with Roosevelt and backed the bill. His overriding goal was to do what was necessary to protect FDR's chances of winning the presidency in 1932 from being harmed by the scandals in New York City. If that meant pursuing the investigations to their final conclusion and bringing public officials to justice, Flynn was willing to spin the wheel.

He did so at considerable risk. Serving as New York's Secretary of State, Flynn was convinced that he was being stalked because of Seabury's not-so-subtle desire to gain the Democratic presidential nomination for himself. "If he [Seabury] could embarrass Roosevelt's Secretary of State," Flynn maintained, "then he thought he could use that as a springboard to the presidency. He searched my records from the time I was born, but he found nothing and he never would admit that he found nothing."

I'm not the most impartial of observers in these matters. Belief in the Democratic Party was ingrained in me as a child, in much the same way that my religious beliefs were. By the time I got to college, and commuted to the same school over the same streets my father had 40 years before, I made it a point to seek every possible opportunity to challenge the Church and Party as corrupt, obsolete institutions, guilty of every sort of transgression. "Every organization is made up of sinners," he told me.

He loved to argue and always encouraged it at the dinner table. As far as he was concerned, I was welcome to my opinions—which he kept telling me, annoyingly, I'd one day outgrow. But no matter what opinions I held, as long as I was living under his roof, I'd register as a Democrat and attend Sunday Mass—"period," as he liked to say. "End of argument. Next case."

* * *

The equation my father helped plant in my head between Catholic Church and Democratic Party meant that I perceived them as fulfilling parallel roles. In my mind, each seemed a source of certainty, a bulwark against evil and exploitation, a guide and protector leading us safely through the perils of today as well as eternity.

My experience of the party was secondhand. I watched my father go out to political dinners and events but rarely accompanied him. I heard the muffled rise and fall of his voice as he rehearsed speeches in his bedroom. I absorbed his faith in the New Deal from his conversations (and sometimes arguments) with friends and acquaintances. Once I heard him say, "It's enough to know that children are poor to know that they need help," and the words stuck with me, resonating with a line from a familiar prayer . . . to Thee do we cry, poor banished children of Eve.

My experience of the Church, in contrast, was up close, intense, personal, and pervasive. For families like mine, in those pre-Vatican II days, life revolved around the Church. The environment was sexually puritanical, ritually demanding, and often stultifying. It was also intensely comforting and secure, liturgically rich, a culture of moral absolutes, theological certainties, and religious devotions in which the answers to all life's questions were readily at hand.

As rigorous and rigid as that culture was, it had, in the form of the Virgin Mary and the saints, a soft center. God the Father was practically unapproachable, the gray-bearded patriarch from the Sistine Chapel, quick to anger and eager to dispatch evildoers to hell. The Virgin Mary was the opposite—patient, understanding, infinitely kind. The *Salve Regina* expressed her attributes best: "O clement, O loving, O sweet Virgin Mary." St. Anthony of Padua was typical of the kind-hearted intercessor who, along with the Virgin, was always there to help people both in their secular and spiritual needs. We prayed to St. Anthony when we lost something. If neither he nor the Virgin could assist, there was St. Jude, the patron of lost causes.

Many Catholics traditionally adopt a particular saint as their own special patron to be prayed to for guidance, protection, and assistance. My father's was Thomas More, the English lawyer and chancellor who was beheaded in 1535 for his refusal to consent to Henry VIII's divorce and remarriage. More was a rarity among saints. He was married and spent his career in public service. My mother's patron was Martin de Porres, a Dominican lay brother who lived in 17th-century Peru. Though he was only "blessed" (one step short of canonization), my mother treated him as the full-fledged saint he would eventually become. Martin was the object of my mother's constant pleas and petitions. She had obtained a relic of him, and when members of her family were sick or dying, the relic was touched to their flesh in hope of a cure. Martin was also odd among saints: He was a black man.

A child's formal introduction to Catholicism was through the Baltimore Catechism. The question-and-answer format was precise and direct. Existence presented basic questions to which God had provided the answers, all of them possessed and guarded by the One True Church. Other religious traditions—Protestant, Jewish, Zoroastrian, take your pick—were gravely deficient. But it was Protestantism and its degenerate and inevitable offspring of religious indifference that presented the real threat.

Unlike Jews or Buddhists, Protestants were interested in claiming our souls and separating us from our faith. They were nowhere near as threatening as Communists, whose object was the violent eradication of religion, but we stayed away from places like the YMCA because we'd been warned of the subtle but ever-present desire of Protestants to convert us. (And, yes, that glistening and seductive swimming pool we glimpsed through its portals seemed a perfect place to find oneself suddenly subjected to a Protestant baptism.)

In early childhood, I was confused by the mention of Protestants, and I wasn't alone. During a lesson about Thanksgiving, Sister Liguori, my second grade teacher, informed us the Pilgrims were Protestants.

A classmate raised his hand. "You mean they were Jews?"

It seemed a fair question. Like Caesar's Gaul, the Bronx we knew was divided into three groups: Italians, Irish, and Jews. If you weren't Catholic, you were Jewish. The Orthodox Jews we sometimes saw on the Grand Concourse or Pelham Parkway wore large black hats similar to the ones worn by the Pilgrims. The Bronx was filled with synagogues. Protestant churches were usually small and tucked away. Yet the near total absence of Protestants and our less-than-clear understanding of who they were (were Presbyterians the same as Protestants?) only served to heighten a sense of their subversive intent.

* * *

I can't recall a single instance of anyone in the neighborhood going over to the Protestant side. My father, on the other hand, in his career as a lawyer and politician, had known Catholics who'd attended "the better" universities, worked at prestigious law firms, married into the upper class, and changed churches. To my father, this was a kind of treason, a bending of belief to ambition, a betrayal that involved class as much as religion. It stirred something visceral inside him.

During his time in Congress, my father developed an acquaintance with a fellow representative, a Republican, who he eventually discovered had been born an Irish Catholic but had traded in his religion, party, and identity for more prestigious and socially advantageous affiliations. In the bar of the Mayflower Hotel, after hearing my father recite a passage from Shakespeare, he said that he found my father "unusually cultured for an Irishman."

"If I thought less of my saliva," my father said, "I'd expectorate in your face."

Those were uncommonly harsh words for my father. He always encouraged us to be respectful of other people, no matter who they were. When it came to those who abandoned their Catholicism to move up the social ladder, however, his feelings reflected a bitter disdain among the Irish that went back to the economic, political, and social benefits conferred on those who took communion in the established church. This act was given an added aura of ignominy during the Famine, when Catholics were converted at the hands of Protestant missionaries in return for a portion of soup.

The actual number of those who took soup (or offered it) was tiny, and far more Protestant clergymen were involved in providing relief than seeking converts. But "taking soup" was a phrase that summed up the continued sense of living in a Protestant country and culture that regarded Catholicism and its adherents as incurably superstitious, ignorant, and alien. The key to survival was loyalty. As well as the supreme virtue of machine politics, loyalty was the bedrock of the Church's power, the cement of neighborhood and family. As Micheal Tuberty has pointed out about Irish-American filmmaker John Ford, "His films lend themselves to a discussion of loyalty, such as the Pacific war and cavalry films and in terms of flaunting the norms of loyalty, such as The Informer." ("Informer"—i.e. the betrayer, the disloyal one—was traditionally the lowest epithet the Irish could hurl at one another.)

* * *

My father made friends easily with Jews and Protestants. He worshipped FDR, an Episcopalian. Baptist Harry Truman was a hero. In his last years, his best friend and golfing companion (and drinking buddy) was an old-line Brooklyn German Protestant named Harry Christman. My father wouldn't join any club that excluded Jews. He was an ecumenicist before the word had any popular currency. When a tiny congregation of Lutherans invited him to attend the dedication of its new church, he readily accepted. The monsignor in charge of our parish heard about it and called to tell my father that, as a prominent Catholic, his participation in such an event might be "a source of scandal to the faithful." My father thanked him for his opinion and went anyway, enjoying, as he described it, "a grand old time."

My father was clear with his children that, by being good Protestants or Jews, adherents of those faiths could enter heaven. But because we'd been born into the Catholic faith, ours was a tougher challenge. We'd been uniquely burdened and uniquely blessed. We had the real presence of Christ in the Eucharist, confession (at once a terrifying and reassuring sacrament that underlined our salvation was always in the balance, capable of being won or lost in a matter of minutes), the saints, and the Virgin Mary, priceless possessions others didn't have. We also had stricter requirements for salvation. The devil had it out for us. He coaxed us to take the easy way out. We were denied the luxury of a death-bed conversion, à la Dutch Schultz, whose baptism in the final moments of his life wiped away his gangster misdeeds and mortal sins.

In the early 1960s, a case came before my father involving a highly decorated Irish-Catholic detective accused of shaking down immigrant doctors who were practicing on their Hispanic clientele without being licensed in New York. If the doctors protested, they were roughed up.

After the detective was convicted, my father was contacted by representatives of several Irish-American organizations—including a monsignor and fellow judge—all echoing the same call for leniency in sentencing. Nobody was killed, the doctors were violating the law, the detective had an outstanding record, and, don't forget, he's one of our own.

Unfortunately for the detective, my father didn't forget. A decade later, a veteran court officer vividly recalled to me how he was in the courtroom the day my father handed down a maximum sentence. In his 30-year career as a court officer, he'd never heard a more fluent and ferocious tongue-lashing than the one my father administered. The detective's crime, my father said, wasn't merely an ordinary instance of racketeering, but an extraordinary betrayal of the public trust and a base and reprehensible repudiation of the immigrant struggle of his own ancestors. The detective learned the hard way that pressing my father's ethno-religious buttons raised rather then lowered the bar.

* * *

My father went to Mass each morning before work. He was punctilious in his devotions, saying the rosary, praying on his knees each night before he went to bed, observing the Lenten fast, and attending the Stations of the Cross. But when it came to the clergy, he was a skeptic, an attitude inherited from his father, who'd faced the efforts of Archbishop Michael Corrigan to stop Catholics from joining the Knights of Labor. When my father thought a priest was an idiot, or a reactionary, or a timeserver, he said so.

In the eighth grade, at St. Raymond's Grammar School, I expressed an interest in studying for the priesthood, a process that in those days began in high school. The priest in charge of vocations pounced on my interest with such enthusiasm that I was afraid to back out or express any doubts. How could I not be honored at the thought of God calling me to be a priest? Yet, at night as I lay awake in bed listening for God's call, all I heard was the soft flow of traffic and the distant rise and fall of police sirens.

Without any encouragement from me, my father bailed me out. He said no, he wouldn't allow me to attend the pre-seminary. When I told the priest what my father said, he was convinced I'd botched the communication. He took it upon himself to contact my father. The gist of what my father told the priest was that no boy of my age had a real clue what he wanted to be. If I had a true vocation, then I'd have it at eighteen, when I got out of high school. Sure enough, by that time, the nighttime voices I heard were sirens of the flesh, succubae whose suggestions were irresistibly seductive.

I never questioned my father about how he reconciled his belief with his anticlericism. We didn't have that type of relationship. He stood off from and above us, and he didn't invite any probing of his personal life. Yet, in retrospect, I think he balanced his faith and his often jaundiced view of those who ran it in much the same way he did his unwavering loyalty to the Democratic Party with his embarrassment or dislike of particular candidates or officeholders.

This was brought home to me on Election Day in 1956. My father was running for a judgeship in the City Court. Adlai Stevenson was the Democratic candidate for president, a fact I was constantly reminded of by the Stevenson pennant my father had tacked over my brother's and my beds. For the first time, he took us into the voting booth with him. Barely looking at the names on the ballot, he pulled all the levers on Row B, voting a straight Democratic ticket.

He told us to remember that the Democratic and Republican parties had, at any one time, roughly the same proportion of fools and knaves. Absolute perfection and moral purity were out of the reach of any individual or party, he said. But each stood for something different, and only together, as a party, as a coherent organization, could people see to it that justice was done for all. "It's the party that matters," he added as we left the polling place, "not the man. You've got to stick with your beliefs." Though he never said so, I'm certain he viewed the Catholic Church in the same light.

* * *

My father went into politics to find work. He graduated from law school in 1929, right in time for the Depression ("the luck of the Irish," he used to sniff), and the first time he got a steady income was when he was elected to the state assembly in 1936. But employment wasn't his only motivation. He inherited a healthy suspicion of great wealth from his father, and the Depression added to that distrust an abiding belief in government's responsibility to protect the non-rich from the failures and excesses of free-market speculation.

As a young lawyer trying to prove himself, he went to the 1932 Democratic Convention in Chicago, not as a delegate but to work behind the scenes for Ed Flynn. The Tammany regulars, upset with Roosevelt's support for the investigations into Mayor Jimmy Walker's administration, hoped to throw the nomination to Al Smith, who was more than willing to accept it. Flynn brought a cadre of Bronx Democrats with him to lobby the delegates and keep them in line for Roosevelt.

My father returned from Chicago more convinced than ever that Roosevelt was the country's best hope. During the campaign of 1932, my father gave speeches for Roosevelt while standing on the back of a flatbed truck that traveled around the Bronx. He wrote a piece of political doggerel that he recited and that he taught me as a child (to me it was poetry, and I still think of it as the first poem I ever learned):

> *A chicken in the pot*
> *is something I ain't got*
> *and I ain't got*
> *two cars in no garage.*
> *The wife ain't wearing silk.*
> *Heck, the kids ain't got no milk,*
> *and today the grocer told me,*
> *"No more charge."*
> *I'm stranded on a rock*
> *and my benny's in the hock[1]*
> *and the thought of winter covers*
> *me with goosepelt.*
> *But there's one thing that I got*
> *Since things ain't been so hot:*
> *I got my mind made up to vote for Roosevelt!*

His friends and acquaintances often remembered my father as "cheerful" or "fun," words that don't immediately pop in to my mind when I think of him. At home, he felt freer to give in to the melancholy and depression that he normally held at bay. But I know where the public image comes from. I only saw him speak in public a few times, but he could move a crowd, make them laugh, and bring them to their feet.

Although the constraints of the Depression forced my parents to postpone their marriage for seven years, each continuing to live at home, my mother never remembered the days of their courtship as grim or despairing. Wherever they went, she said, whether it was a political function or a parish dance, "Your father was always the life of the party."

[1]
"Benny" was New York slang for an overcoat. It probably derives from the Irish word báinín (pron. baaneen), or jacket or overcoat made of homespun woolen cloth.

I GAVE A MAN !

SALVATORE J. LaGUMINA

FAITH, POWER, AND IDENTITY

CATHOLICS IN NEW YORK POLITICS

Politics, it has been observed, is the field in which society carries out conflict by means other than war. Ethnic politics, furthermore, reflects society's tendency to divide itself into competing groups embracing the particular interests and concerns of racial, national, and religious groups, usually minorities. This phenomenon has been evident in New York City throughout most of its history and has particular resonance when it comes to Catholics in politics.

However, it would be wrong to conclude that there was a unified Catholic response to the contest for political power in New York. Ethnic tensions among Italians, Irish, and Germans—the three largest Catholic ethnic groups—gave lie to the nativist fantasy of a pan-Catholic political movement. What's more, Catholics did not always march in step with their bishops on political issues. Newspaper publisher Patrick Ford (1837–1913), an Irish-Catholic immigrant who founded the *Irish World* in 1870, criticized the church for not supporting his call for greater labor militancy. John Purroy Mitchel (1879–1918), a devout Catholic who served as the "boy mayor" of New York from 1914 to 1917, fell out with much of the Catholic establishment after he criticized the church's involvement and favoritism in municipal politics. Even more extreme in rejecting the church's lead was Elizabeth Gurley Flynn (1890–1964), a descendant of a long line of Irish revolutionaries and a leading militant labor protagonist who became a staunch Communist.

Indeed, it was on issues of capital and labor that some New York Catholic politicians split with the Church's more moderate positions. Congressman Vito Marcantonio (1902–1954), who represented East Harlem in the House of Representatives in the 1930s and 1940s, was a leftist who was investigated by the FBI for his supposed socialist and communist sympathies. And yet, he also marched in East Harlem's religious processions, and he was member of the Holy Name Society at the time of his death in 1954. Notwithstanding Marcantonio's displays of piety, Cardinal Francis Spellman refused his family permission for a Catholic funeral.

That diversity of opinion would have surprised the church's non-Catholic critics in the middle of the 19th century, when Catholics began arriving in New York in great numbers. Nativists saw New York Catholicism as a monolith and its adherents as intellectual and political slaves of the Pope. Tammany Hall, however, saw the new arrivals not as people to be scorned, condemned, or judged but as potential voters. Irish Catholics began arriving in the 1820s and 1830s, just as New York embarked on massive public-works projects, including construction of the Erie Canal and the Croton Aqueduct.[1] Tammany, an arm of the city's Democratic Party, found many of these Catholic immigrants jobs as marshals, street inspectors, health wardens, and lamplighters, provided they voted Democratic regularly and often.[2]

These developments notwithstanding, anti-Catholic bigotry in city politics persisted with the emergence of staunchly nativist movements in the 1830s, the elections of nativists Aaron Clark (1784–1861) and James Harper (1795–1869) as mayor in 1837 and 1844, respectively, and the creation in 1845 of the even more rabid Native American Party.

Tammany, on the other hand, opened its ranks to these new voters through an elaborate network of auxiliaries and clubs that made the Democratic Party perhaps the most representative political organization in the city. Irish Catholics responded to these overtures with alacrity and aplomb. They grasped the notion that politics was the way to get ahead, the means by which they could overcome the obstacles of poverty and discrimination. Many of them possessed some innate advantages later Catholic groups lacked. They spoke English, were accustomed to forms of representative government, and had familiarity with the mechanics of elections, the role of the press, and political organization, among other things.[3] The Irish's political ascendancy was matched by their growing influence and steadfastness in the American Catholic Church, a loyalty that was soon rewarded by prominence in the church hierarchy.

In 1842, Irish-born John Hughes (1797–1864) became bishop of New York, a milestone not only for Catholics but for the city itself. Over the next 20-plus years, Hughes battled openly with nativist politicians and created a vibrant Catholic presence in New York, opening doz-

1
Edward R. Ellis, *The Epic of New York City* (New York: Coward-McCann, 1966), 227.
2
Ibid., 234, 246.
3
Denis W. Brogan, *Politics in America* (New York: Doubleday, 1960), 85.

TOP

Thomas Nast (1840–1902), *The Economical Council in Albany, New York,* wood engraving, published in *Vogue,* 1869
Cartoonist Nast skewered both his adversaries by dressing New York Tammany politicians in the vestments of the Roman Catholic hierarchy on the occasion of the opening of the First Vatican Council, the Church's 20th ecumenical council, in December 1869. Boss Tweed became a bishop and Governor Hoffman became "Pius Hoffman I."

BOTTOM LEFT

George Hayward, [Tammany Hall], 1830, lithograph, for *D. T. Valentine's Manual for 1858*
Tammany Hall served as the clubhouse for both the Society of Saint Tammany (or Columbian Order), a fraternal group founded in 1789, and the Tammany Hall wing of the Democratic Party.

BOTTOM RIGHT

[The sachems of Tammany Hall], 1929
The group of Tammany officials included Catholic mayor James J. Walker, second from left, and four-time governor of New York and 1928 Democratic presidential candidate Alfred E. Smith, at the right, wearing his trademark derby.

THE TIGER'S SHARE

TAMMANY—" I'm monarch of all I survey,
My rule there is none to dispute.
From Harlem right down to the bay
I'm lord of the man and the brute.

TOP

H. Gillam, *The Tiger's Share*, c. 1890, color lithograph
In the Tweed era and afterwards, cartoonists associated Tammany Democracy with the tiger.

RIGHT TOP

Programs for James Dunphy Association Annual Ball at Irving Hall, January 29, 1872, and the Annual Excursion of the Thomas Coman Association to Dudley's Grove, August 14, 1871
Democratic politicians supported one another, with James Dunphy serving as president of the Thomas Coman Association.

RIGHT BOTTOM

M. T. Brennan Coterie invitation and dance card, 1870, paper; gelatin silver prints on printing-out paper; gilt cord
Supporters of Tammany Hall politicians such as Matthew T. Brennan organized local social activities and fundraisers honoring their patrons.

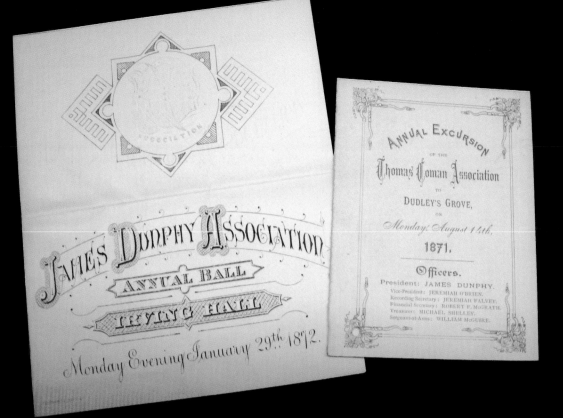

JAMES DUNPHY ASSOCIATION
ANNUAL BALL
IRVING HALL
Monday Evening January 29th 1872.

ANNUAL EXCURSION
OF THE
Thomas Coman Association
TO
DUDLEY'S GROVE,
ON
Monday, August 14th,
1871.

Officers.
President: JAMES DUNPHY.
Vice-President: JEREMIAH O'BRIEN.
Recording Secretary: JEREMIAH FALVEY.
Financial Secretary: ROBERT F. McGRATH.
Treasurer: MICHAEL SHELLEY.
Sergeant-at-Arms: WILLIAM McGUIRE.

M. T. Brennan
COTERIE
ACADEMY OF MUSIC
Wednesday, January 12th,
1870.

M. T. BRENNAN
COTERIE
Academy of Music
Wednesday Evening
JAN. 12
1870

LEFT

Thomas A. Sindelar (1867–1923), Lotos Club State Dinner Honoring Alfred E. Smith menu cover, March 29, 1919, photogravure, with multiple autographs

Smith won his first gubernatorial election in 1918. New York's Lotos Club honored him with a dinner early in his term.

TOP RIGHT

Medallic Art Company, William Russell Grace commemorative medal, 1980, bronze

In 1880, New York City elected its first Catholic mayor, shipping magnate William R. Grace (1831–1904).

MIDDLE RIGHT

Byron Co., [Richard Croker and Companions], 1899, gelatin silver print on printing-out paper

Richard Croker (1843–1922), an Irish Protestant by birth, became a Catholic convert when he entered politics. By 1886, he controlled Tammany Hall; abroad from 1894–1897, he resumed control in 1897, which he retained until 1901.

BOTTOM RIGHT

Brown Brothers, *Charles F. Murphy* (1858–1924), undated, gelatin silver print

Leader of Tammany Hall from 1902–1924, Murphy was the city's most powerful political figure.

ens of new churches, bringing to the diocese ten new religious communities, and expanding Catholic educational and charitable activities. Hughes was the first New York archbishop to become a national political figure—as an aggressive defender of Catholicism at a time of virulent anti-Catholicism, he was not one to shy away from controversy. His most famous political foray involved the Catholic schools he was building. He proposed that these religious schools should receive taxpayer support, a stance that outraged non-Catholics. When the City Council refused Hughes's demand, he denounced the Protestant-dominated Public School Society, which administered the city's public schools and assigned textbooks that demeaned Catholics, and founded an ad-hoc slate of candidates pledged to support his position. Historian Edward R. Ellis has argued that this was the first and only time in American history that Catholics formed their own political party and mounted a slate of candidates that openly supported the church's positions on a political issue.[4] Although Hughes's party failed to elect a single nominee, the effort served to convince Tammany Hall that Catholics were a political force in the making.

William M. Tweed (1823–1878), legendary boss of Tammany Hall in the middle of the 19th century, effectively harnessed Catholic political power by obtaining Irish backing of his political machine for mutual gain. Among the Catholics who became prominent in Tweed's organization were Peter B. Sweeney, city chamberlain who controlled the judiciary, Richard B. Connolly, city comptroller, Matthew T. Brennan, sheriff, and John H. McCann, judge of the superior court.[5]

Tammany's willingness to embrace and even comfort Catholic immigrants laid the groundwork for Irish domination of the city's political scene by the late 19th century. With new-found stability, thanks to politics, came economic and cultural accomplishment: in 1890, some 30 percent of New York City's teachers were Irish women, and the Irish literacy rate exceeded 90 percent.

After the fall of Boss Tweed in 1871, former Congressman "Honest John" Kelly became the first Catholic leader of Tammany Hall. Less than a decade later, in 1880, the city elected its first Catholic mayor, shipping magnate William R. Grace (1831–1904). He was a daily communicant and a philanthropist who won admiration for establishing the Grace Institute, which provided free tuition for women who sought to learn career skills. With the rise to power of Kelly and Grace, Catholics assumed control of city politics, and for the next half century Irish Americans dominated Tammany Hall and the city's top political offices.

Although the urban machine was associated with corruption and vice, it also produced voices—Catholic voices—that challenged the nation's belief in laissez-faire economics and a society based on Protestant Yankee notions of rugged individualism. That critique led two extraordinary New York Catholic politicians to bring about enormous social and political

4
Ellis, *Epic of New York City,* 254.
5
Ibid., 335.

reforms in the first quarter of the 20th century. They were Charles Francis Murphy (1858–1924), the head of Tammany Hall during much of that period, and Governor Alfred E. Smith (1873–1944).

Murphy, the son of immigrants, ran a popular saloon on the East Side. Saloons were common meeting places for Tammany's leaders, serving as clubhouses where important contacts were made and all sorts of jobs or favors were dispensed. Through the contacts he made, Murphy became a major factor in New York politics. Although the only official position he ever held was that of dock commissioner, he was, by virtue of his leadership of Tammany from 1902 to 1924, the city's most powerful political figure. He mentored and promoted Smith, who became one of the early 20th century's most effective reformers, pushing laws that improved worker safety, building a safety net for the sick and unemployed, and taking measures to protect children against the market's exploitation. These efforts followed up on Pope Leo XIII's 1891 encyclical, *Rerum novarum*, which exhorted employers to respect the rights of workers. But Smith also welcomed the advice and expertise of socially minded non-Catholics, including Frances Perkins (1880–1965), Robert Moses (1888–1981), and Belle Moskowitz (1877–1933).

The city's Irish took special pride in Smith, who went on to become the first Catholic presidential nominee in 1928 after a sterling career as a four-term governor of New York. Little known at the time was the fact that one of Smith's grandfathers was born in Italy.

Italian Americans constitute another important source of Catholic political power, especially in the 20th century. Not all Italians were Catholic of course—the best known Italian-American political figure in New York in the 1930s and 1940s was Mayor Fiorello H. La Guardia (1882–1947), son of a Protestant father and a Jewish mother.

Italian-American influence on city politics was first evident around the turn of the last century, when Italian names began appearing as nominees for minor city posts, such as coroner. Surprisingly, despite the proletarian background of many Italian Catholic immigrants and their children, more than a few joined the Republican Party (the most prominent spokesman of which in the city was, in fact, Fiorello La Guardia). A number of factors may help explain why Italians did not fully embrace the Democrats, who held power because of their willingness to embrace ethnic and religious minorities. The party was dominated by Irish Americans, some of whom froze out Italians—never mind that they were Catholics, too. La Guardia's success in the Republican Party also was an attraction at a time when ideology was not a paramount consideration—La Guardia may have been a Republican, but he was also, in essence, a New Dealer.

TOP RIGHT
Alfred E. Smith campaign buttons, 1920s

TOP LEFT
Brown derby, fur felt with grosgrain
ribbon, Knox New York, with simulated
signature "Alfred E. Smith" stamped
on interior sweatband, 1928–1944
Alfred E. Smith used the brown derby
as his trademark during his 1928
presidential campaign.

BOTTOM
[Alfred E. Smith casting his ballot in
his first race for governor], 1918,
gelatin silver print

TOP

Paul MacGahan, [Laying the cornerstone of the Columbus Monument, Columbus Circle], September 16, 1892

BOTTOM LEFT

John Albok, [Congressman Vito Marcantonio at World War II Victory rally], 1943, gelatin silver print

BOTTOM RIGHT

George Grantham Bain, [Elizabeth Gurley Flynn (Mrs. J.A. Jones)], c. 1919

Flynn (1890–1964), a self-described "rebel girl," organized labor, helped found the American Civil Liberties Union, and led the American Communist Party.

Despite the hostility of some Irish Catholics toward newcomers, Tammany Hall as an institution was aware of the power of Italian votes and sought to win them over. One of the earliest examples of this outreach, and of growing Italian voting strength, took place around 1892 as the city prepared to celebrate the 400th anniversary of Christopher Columbus's journey to the New World. To commemorate the event, the city unveiled a new statue of Columbus by the southwest corner of Central Park. Previously, the city's Italian community had gathered around the statue of Giuseppe Garibaldi, leader of Italian unification and opponent of the Catholic Church, in Washington Square Park. But after 1892, they adopted Columbus, a pious Catholic, as a rallying figure.

In 1909, thanks to legislation sponsored by two Tammany stalwarts—Al Smith, then a state assemblyman, and State Senator "Big Tim" Sullivan (1863–1913)—New York designated Columbus Day a state holiday. To say that Tammany Hall was trying to curry favor with New York Italian Americans is to state the obvious. But it did help keep the bulk of Italian Catholic voters from straying to the Republican Party.[6]

The city's most prominent Italian Catholic politician of the immediate postwar era was Vincent Impellitteri (1900–1987), a native of Sicily. He was elected president of the City Council in 1945 and 1949, and while in office his staunch anticommunism put him in good stead with Cardinal Francis Spellman. In 1947 and 1948, Impellitteri urged his Italian-American constituents to advise relatives in Italy to vote against the Communist Party, which was making inroads in postwar Italian politics.

In some respects, the special mayoral election in 1950 (to complete the term of Irish Catholic William O'Dwyer, who had resigned) marked the political coming-of-age for Italians in New York: all three candidates were Italian immigrants. Two of them were Catholic: Edward Corsi, the Republican candidate, and Impellitteri, who ran on his own line, the Experience Party. The Democratic candidate, Ferdinand Pecora, was Protestant. (After Tammany Hall, under the leadership of its first Italian boss, Carmine De Sapio, chose Pecora as its candidate, the spurned Impellitteri formed his own party.) With the votes split three ways, Impellitteri became the city's first Italian Catholic mayor.

Catholic influence on city politics has been profound, both in terms of raw political power and in the implementation of policies that changed the relationship between government and the people. The Catholic political journey affirmed the axiom that, in America, politics is a matter of interests and personalities.[7] To describe a New York politician as "Catholic" is a dangerous business, because Catholic politicians have never fit neatly into one category or party. Some used their political positions for personal gain, while others advocated for the poor and powerless—Catholic and non-Catholic alike. Some did both. While that was

6
Salvatore LaGumina, "Columbus Day: A Rallying Point For Italian Americans," ECCSA Journal 11, no. 1 (winter 1996): 60–71.

7
Brogan, Politics, 41.

TOP

Campaign banners, New York, 1945
The banners show the 1945 Democratic
ticket: Irish Catholic William O'Dwyer
for mayor; Lazarus Joseph, a Jewish
candidate for comptroller; Vincent
Impellitteri, an Italian Catholic for City
Council president.

BOTTOM

Alfred Aidala, [Vincent Impellitteri
greeting the crowd following his
election victory], November 8, 1950,
gelatin silver print

and is true of politicians in general, the Catholic political journey in New York is important because of the key role politics played in creating a space for Catholics to build on their immigrant dreams.

The history of New York Catholics in politics underscores the diversity of opinions and personalities within the Catholic community. It also shows the ways in which Catholic politicians balanced ethnicity and faith to achieve power and influence through the ballot box.

EDWARD T. O'DONNELL

SOGGARTH AROON

THE RISE AND FALL OF
REV. EDWARD McGLYNN

1
The New York Times, June 19, 1887.

On June 18, 1887, thousands of protesters paraded through the streets of lower Manhattan near Union Square. Nearly all the participants were members of labor unions, political clubs, ethnic associations, and reform societies. The loudest cheers from the throngs of onlookers were reserved for the 1,500 members of St. Stephen's parish, for the parade was organized on their behalf. The signs they held aloft told their story: "Our purses will be opened when our pastor is restored," "We are loyal Catholics and loyal Americans," and "Tammany Hall can never crush our glorious Fr. McGlynn."[1]

The rally was protesting the suspension and impending excommunication of Reverend Edward McGlynn, a priest who had earned a reputation over the preceding decade as a vociferous champion of the poor and espouser of radical social ideology. In an archdiocese known for its authoritarian hierarchy, the mass rally in support of McGlynn was an event without precedent and one that revealed the many conflicting interests and concerns that challenged the Catholic Church in New York during the Gilded Age.

Edward McGlynn, the seventh child of Donegal immigrants Peter and Sarah McGlynn, was born on September 27, 1837, in New York City. Unlike so many of the Irish that surrounded them, the McGlynns lived in middle-class comfort, as Peter ran a successful contracting business. In 1851, the year following Edward's graduation from the Free Academy (later renamed City College), he was selected to study at the Urban College of the Propaganda in Rome as preparation for entering the priesthood. After nine years of study in which he

147

distinguished himself as a scholar, speaker, and student leader, he earned his doctorate in philosophy and sacred theology and was ordained in March 1860.[2]

Returning to New York to begin work as a parish priest, McGlynn reported to St. Joseph's Church in Greenwich Village. There, he fell in with a circle of liberal priests called the "Accademia" that met regularly to discuss "untouchable" subjects such as celibacy, papal authority, the Latin Mass, religious orders, and parochial schools. While the group eventually disbanded under pressure from the archdiocese leadership, the friends McGlynn made and the radical perspective he developed as a member stayed with him for the rest of his life.[3]

After short stints at St. Brigid's, St. James's, St. Ann's, and a makeshift chapel at the military hospital in Central Park at the end of the Civil War, McGlynn was appointed assistant pastor at St. Stephen's church on East 29th Street in 1865. Within a year, he was named pastor, a position he was to hold for the next 22 years.[4]

From the very outset of his tenure at St. Stephen's, McGlynn distinguished himself as a socially liberal and independent-minded cleric, dedicated to aiding the poor and helpless of his parish. McGlynn did not have to look far to find them, for St. Stephen's was one of the largest and poorest parishes in the city. From all accounts, McGlynn's tireless efforts gained him the undying admiration of his parishioners. Many took to referring to him as *soggarth aroon*, Irish for "precious priest."[5]

Significantly, McGlynn never opened a parochial school. Nor did he ever attempt to do so, even though successive archbishops beginning in 1842 had made establishing parochial schools a priority second only to building more churches. McGlynn's resistance on this issue indicated his support for one of the key ideas of an emerging liberal Catholicism: that American Catholics would be better served by entering the American mainstream rather than by maintaining the defensive and inward-looking separatist ethos they understandably developed in the mid 19th century in response to nativist hostility.[6]

The plight of his flock was never far from McGlynn's mind. He wrote of the "never ending procession of men, women, and children" who came knocking on his door, "begging not so much for alms as for employment...and personally appealing to me to obtain for them an opportunity of working for their daily bread.... I began to ask myself, 'Is there no remedy? Is this God's order that the poor shall by constantly becoming poorer in all our large cities, the world over?'"[7]

McGlynn believed he found that remedy in 1881, when he received a copy of a new book, *Progress and Poverty*, by Henry George (1839–1897), a man fast emerging as one of the

2
Stephen Bell, *Rebel, Priest, and Prophet: A Biography of Dr. Edward McGlynn* (New York: Devin-Adair, 1937), 5–6.

3
Robert Emmett Curran, "Prelude to 'Americanism': The New York Accademia and Clerical Radicalism in the Late Nineteenth Century," *Church History* 47, no. 1 (March 1978): 48–65.

4
Bell, *Rebel, Priest, and Prophet*, 9–11; Leonard J. Hunt, *St. Stephen's Parish, Our Hundred Years, 1848–1948* (New York: n.p., 1948).

5
James Gilhooley, "Soggarth Aroon, 'The Precious Priest,'" *America*, March 19, 1983, 205–207.

6
Jay Dolan, *The Immigrant Church: New York's Irish and German Catholics, 1815–1865* (New York: Doubleday, 1985), 99–120; Richard Shaw, *Dagger John: The Unquiet Life and Times of Archbishop John Hughes* (New York: Paulist Press, 1977), 139–175.

7
Sylvester L. Malone, *Dr. Edward McGlynn* (New York: McAuliffe and Booth, 1918), 106.

CHURCH OF SAINT STEPHEN.

42   EAST TWENTY-EIGHTH STREET.

PAGE 146

St. Stephen's church, New York, c. 1870, engraving, published in *Frank Leslie's Illustrated*

Father McGlynn employed Italian painter Constantino Brumidi (1805–1880) to decorate the church interior.

TOP LEFT

Dr. Edward McGlynn (1837-1900), c. 1870, from John Gilmary Shea, editor, *The Catholic Churches of New York City* (New York: Lawrence G. Goulding & Co., 1878)

McGlynn became pastor of St. Stephen's in 1866.

TOP RIGHT

Church of Saint Stephen, East Twenty-Eighth Street, 1878, from John Gilmary Shea, editor, *The Catholic Churches of New York City* (New York: Lawrence G. Goulding & Co., 1878)

BOTTOM

Rev. Dr. Edward McGlynn, c. 1896, from Moses King, *Notable New Yorkers of 1896-1899* (New York; Boston, 1899)

From 1895 until his death, McGlynn served as pastor of St. Mary's Roman Catholic Church, Newburgh, New York.

REV. DR. EDWARD McGLYNN

FORMER PASTOR

ST. STEPHEN'S CHURCH (ROMAN CATHOLIC)

149

TOP

**First Labor Day Parade, Union Square,
1882, from** *Frank Leslie's Illustrated*
More than 30,000 Knights of Labor and
craft union members responded to a call
issued by New York City's Central Labor
Union to march in support of an eight-
hour workday and other labor demands.

RIGHT

W. T. Smedley (1858-1920), *In Mulberry
Bend, 1893,* **published in** *Harper's
Monthly,* **June 1894**
New York's teeming immigrant
neighborhoods housed workers who
responded to McGlynn's speeches.

FOLLOWING SPREAD

C. J. Taylor, *Between Two Popes,* **published
in** *Puck,* **January 19, 1887**
McGlynn is depicted between the figures
of Pope Leo XIII and Henry George (also
dressed in papal garb). In his hand he
holds a summons from Rome, which,
by refusing to answer, ultimately cost
him his parish.

IN MULBERRY BEND.

nation's best-known social reformers and critics of laissez-faire industrial capitalism. In vivid, apocalyptic language that invoked the moral authority of both the Founding Fathers and Jesus Christ, the book warned that growing social inequality threatened American democracy and republican values. "This association of poverty with progress," asserted George, "is the great enigma of our times." George identified land monopoly as the cause of social inequality and proposed a "single-tax" that effectively abolished private property but preserved the virtues of the capitalist system. The book became a bestseller among workers and middle-class reformers.[8]

The book appealed to McGlynn as "a poem of philosophy, a prophesy and a prayer." Suddenly, he had found the solution to the riddle of why poverty grew worse even as the nation experienced remarkable material progress. McGlynn soon became George's most zealous champion. But unbeknownst to him, church officials in America and Rome were already considering putting *Progress and Poverty* on the Vatican's *Index Librorum Prohibitorum*, or List of Prohibited Books.[9]

Remarkably, the first outlet for McGlynn's budding radicalism was the Irish Land League, which flourished between 1879 and 1883. Irish nationalism surged in the late 1870s, when Ireland plunged into a serious agricultural crisis and thousands faced starvation and eviction. Founded by nationalist Michael Davitt in 1879, the league demanded major reform of Ireland's landlord-dominated land system.[10]

The movement quickly spread to the United States, where by 1882 activists established nearly 1,000 American Land League branches, from major cities such as New York and Chicago to the mining districts in Pennsylvania and Butte, and raised more than $500,000. In contrast to earlier nationalist activity, the league became a mass movement, rather than an obsession of a small band of diehards. Its members included upper-class professionals and poor factory workers alike. It even included many priests—quite remarkable given the long-standing hostility of the Catholic Church toward nationalist movements.

While many Irish Americans joined the league out of devotion to Ireland, many like McGlynn did so because they were drawn to the movement's social radicalism. Henry George, for example, was neither Irish nor Catholic, but he joined the league. He and McGlynn saw in the condemnation of landlord exploitation in Ireland an effective critique of industrial capitalism in the United States. Patrick Ford, the Irish-born editor of the *Irish World and Industrial Liberator*, the nation's largest-selling Irish weekly, shared this view. "[T]he struggle in Ireland," he frequently reminded his readers, "is radically and essentially the same as the struggle in America—a contest against legalized forms of oppression."[12]

8

Henry George, *Progress and Poverty: An Inquiry into the Cause of Industrial Depressions and of Increase of Want with Increase of Wealth* (New York: Random House, 1939), 9–10. For more on Henry George, see Charles Albro Barker, *Henry George* (New York: Oxford, 1955), and Edward T. O'Donnell, *Talisman of a Lost Hope: Henry George and Gilded Age America* (New York: Columbia University Press, forthcoming).

9

Malone, 106.

10

Thomas N. Brown, *Irish-American Nationalism, 1870–1890* (New York: J. B. Lippincott, 1966), 80–103.

11

For information regarding League financial reports and the number of branches, see *Irish-American*, March 19, 1881, 5; April 9, 1881, 8; June 4, 1881, 5; June 25, 1881, 5; July 22, 1882, 5; October 21, 1882, 4; *Irish Nation*, February 4, 1882, 8; March 4, 1882, 2; April 15, 1882, 2; *Irish World*, February 16, 1884.

12

Irish World, December 31, 1881, 4. See also Eric Foner, "Class, Ethnicity, and Radicalism in the Gilded Age: The Land League and Irish America," in his *Politics and Ideology in the Age of the Civil War* (New York: Oxford University Press, 1980), and James P. Rodechko, *Patrick Ford and His Search for America: A Case Study of Irish American Journalism, 1870–1913* (New York: Arno Press, 1976).

McGlynn emerged as an important and revered speaker at Land League rallies in New York. He was not afraid to express his radicalism in blunt terms. "If I had to choose between Land-lordism and Communism," he told a rapt audience at a rally in Union Square in August 1882, "I would prefer the latter…. It is intended for the welfare of the masses." [13]

Unfortunately for McGlynn, the speech gained the attention of Cardinal McCloskey and, more ominously, authorities in Rome. In the 1880s, Church officials on both sides of the Atlantic had grown increasingly concerned about the influence of radicalism on American Catholics, specifically the works of Henry George and the rise of the massive industrial union the Knights of Labor. Cardinal John McCloskey resisted Rome's urging that he silence McGlynn and instead secured from him a promise not to speak at any more Land League rallies. [14]

In the fall of 1882, McGlynn met George for the first time, and each took an instant liking to the other. "Already captured by *Progress and Poverty*," remembered McGlynn, "I was now captured by its author." George wrote that he quickly "learned to reverence his [McGlynn's] deep and inostentatious piety, his broad Catholic spirit, and his devotion to the cause of the poor." This meeting marked the beginning of a long and fruitful relationship. [15]

Their big moment came in 1886, when public officials in New York (indeed, nationwide) responded to a record numbers of strikes and boycotts by arresting more than 100 labor leaders. Outraged, the city's Central Labor Union (an organization spawned by the Land League in 1882) established the United Labor Party and nominated Henry George as their candidate for mayor. [16]

McGlynn was thrilled by the prospect of a George candidacy, but his support for the radical reformer soon brought him into conflict with the new archbishop, the ultraconservative Michael A. Corrigan (1839–1902), who placed a high premium on priestly obedience and opposed anything that smacked of heresy or communism. Corrigan ordered McGlynn not to campaign for George, but the radical priest stuck to his principles. "I, in view of my rights and duties as a citizen, which were not surrendered when I became a priest, am determined to do what I can to support Mr. George," he wrote in remarkably defiant terms, "and I am also stimulated by love for the poor and oppressed laboring classes, which seems particular-ly consonant with the charitable and philanthropic character of the priesthood." [17]

McGlynn's defiance earned him a suspension from his priestly duties for two weeks, but he continued to appear in public with George. McGlynn's identification with the labor cam-paign, even though silent, became crucial as church officials began to openly condemn George and his teachings. [18]

13
Irish World, July 1, 1882, 3. See also *Irish World*, July 8 and 15, 1882, 1; January 6, 1883, 8; *Irish American*, March 27, 1880, 4; *The New York Times*, February 27, 1883, 8.

14
Bell, *Rebel, Priest, and Prophet*, 29; Henry J. Browne, *The Catholic Church and the Knights of Labor* (Washington, D.C.: Catho-lic University Press, 1949), passim.

15
Henry George Jr., *The Life of Henry George*, vol. 9 of *The Complete Works of Henry George*, 10 vols. (Garden City, N.Y.: Fels Fund Library Edition, 1906–1911), 402; *The Standard*, January 8, 1887, 1.

16
For an excellent article on the election of 1886, see David Scobey, "Boycotting the Politics Factory: Labor Radicalism and the New York City Mayoral Election of 1884 [sic]," *Radical History Review* 28–30 (1984): 280–325.

17
Letter of McGlynn to Corrigan, September 29, 1886, quoted in Bell, *Rebel, Priest, and Prophet*, 34; Robert E. Curran, *Michael Augustine Corrigan and the Shaping of Conservative Catholicism in America, 1878–1902* (New York: Arno Press, 1978), 196–197.

18
The Standard, January 8, 1887, 2.

AJAX DEFYING THE LIGHTNING.
A NEW ATTRACTION AT THE GEORGE-M'GLYNN SHOW.

TOP

Henry George for Mayor of Greater New York, 1897; Memorial button, 1897; lithographed metal

Single-tax advocate Henry George (1839–1897) ran unsuccessfully for mayor of New York in 1886 with McGlynn's support. George ran again in 1897, but died before Election Day.

BOTTOM LEFT

Archbishop Michael Augustine Corrigan, D.D., 1897, frontispiece photogravure, from *Celebration of the Episcopal Jubilee of The Most Reverend Michael Augustine Corrigan, D.D. ...*(1898)

Liberal McGlynn and conservative Archbishop Corrigan collided over McGlynn's support for Henry George's politics, which were condemned as heretical.

BOTTOM RIGHT

***Ajax Defying The Lightning: A New Attraction at the George-M'Glynn Show,* c. 1887, engraving**

Dr. McGlynn's continued support of Henry George resulted first in his removal as pastor of St. Stephen's and then in his excommunication.

155

TOP LEFT

Frederick Opper, "Cold, bitter cold!"
from *Puck*, January 1888

Support for McGlynn and his Anti-
Poverty Society declined following
his excommunication.

TOP RIGHT

Anti-Poverty Society souvenir, 1887

As "the people's priest" and president
of the Anti-Poverty Society, McGlynn
attracted crowds to his weekly Sunday
night revival-style meetings with calls
for social justice.

BOTTOM

"The Power Behind The Pope," from
Judge, February 1887

Judge supported McGlynn; in its view,
Tammany Hall, which lost votes to George
in the 1886 campaign, was the power
behind church authorities.

The latter effort took an astonishingly bold turn a few days before the election when one of Corrigan's lieutenants, Vicar General Monsignor Thomas Preston, provided Tammany Hall with a letter condemning George's ideas as heretical. Tammany made thousands of copies of the letter and distributed them to Catholics as they left church on the Sunday before the election. "They think his principles unsound and unsafe, and contrary to the teachings of the church," Monsignor Preston wrote, speaking for the archdiocese's clergy.[19]

On Election Day, George outpolled the Republican candidate, the 27-year-old Theodore Roosevelt, but lost narrowly to Tammany Democrat Abram Hewitt. George and his supporters, such as McGlynn, hoped this strong showing was the sign of greater things to come, perhaps even the establishment of a national reform or labor party and a presidential campaign in 1888.[20]

But within months, the United Labor Party began to splinter, and McGlynn found himself under the archbishop's heel. The latter ordeal began to unfold in January when, at the request of Corrigan, the Vatican called McGlynn to Rome. McGlynn refused to go, and Corrigan removed him as pastor at St. Stephen's. Corrigan lobbied Rome even more vigorously to have McGlynn severely disciplined, if not excommunicated, and George's works placed on the *Index*. "Georgean economics are a civil disease bordering on madness," he wrote to Cardinal Simeoni, prefect of *Propaganda Fide* in Rome. He asserted that McGlynn believed that "the savior of society is not our beloved [Pope] Leo but his friend George, pontiff of a democratic church without dominion or tiara."[21]

The struggle between McGlynn, the representative of the liberal wing of the Catholic Church, and Archbishop Corrigan, the paragon of conservative, ultramontane clericalism, was no mere local affair. It both represented and deeply influenced a similar debate raging at the national level—namely, that over the right of Catholics to be members of labor unions (in particular, the Knights of Labor) and to embrace social and economic reforms. It was soon transformed into an unprecedented episode of antiauthoritarian protest by the working-class parishioners of St. Stephen's.[22]

Two days after Corrigan removed McGlynn as pastor, more than 7,000 protesters gathered at the church and established a formal boycott of the parish. That same evening, they held a mass rally, where speakers voiced a consistent theme upholding clerical authority in religious matters but vehemently denouncing the use of such authority to suppress the political activism of Catholic priests and laymen. Union leader John Bealin drew a clear parallel between abusive employers and an abusive hierarchy. "When men attempt to better their condition by organizing their trade they are blacklisted, they are driven from the shop and the streetcar; and now we see a priest, the only one among the thousand who dare to speak the truth, struck down by his superiors," he said.[23] Demonstrations continued on a nightly

19
Bell, *Rebel, Priest, and Prophet,* 35; Curran, *Michael Augustine Corrigan,* 196–197.

20
For full details on the campaign results, see Louis F. Post and Fred C. Leubuscher, *Henry George's 1886 Campaign: An Account of the George-Hewitt Campaign in the New York Municipal Election of 1886* (New York: n.p., 1887).

21
The Standard, January 8, 1887, 1–2; January 15, 1887, 1; February 5, 1887, 1; *New York Tribune,* November 26, 1886; Barker, *Henry George,* 487–90; Curran, *Michael Augustine Corrigan,* 203–215.

22
James F. Donnelly, "Catholic New Yorkers and New York Socialists, 1870–1920," Ph. D. diss., New York University, 1982, 89–132.

23
The Standard, January 22, 1887, 1; *New York Tribune,* January 17, 1887; Curran, *Michael Augustine Corrigan,* 220–223.

basis at St. Stephen's, and the boycott of the collection plate caused contributions to the debt-ridden church to plummet.

To provide himself with an alternative pulpit, McGlynn soon founded a group called the Anti-Poverty Society. In late March, before a crowd of thousands at the Academy of Music on 14th Street, McGlynn gave what became his most famous speech, "The Cross of the New Crusade." In compelling oratorical style, McGlynn called for joining Christian morality with secular reform to bring social justice to the suffering masses. No longer could Christianity be a faith concerned only with the next life, argued McGlynn. The Anti-Poverty Society be- gan holding weekly Sunday-evening revival-style meetings and soon drew crowds of 2,000 to 3,000 people. Alarmed, Corrigan soon forbade Catholics from attending the meetings, even going so far as to deny two people Catholic burials on account of their participation.[24]

The creation of the Anti-Poverty Society, with its explicit message of social justice and oppo- sition to hierarchical authority, and the radical agitation of the poor parishioners at St. Stephen's were events unprecedented in the history of the archdiocese. They cheered those who viewed the Church as a major obstacle to future efforts by working-class Catholics to come to terms with the jarring changes being brought about by Gilded Age industrial capitalism. Here, New York Catholics were making a profound statement: They would not choose between their worlds of faith and of work. They would remain good Catholics—after all, they were demanding the *reinstatement* of their pastor—while at the same time affiliating with a secular movement aimed at bettering their earthly condition. "I think they will have to excommunicate one or two besides Dr. McGlynn," mused one official of the Anti-Poverty Society. "They will have to excommunicate some millions of American Catholics."[25]

On July 3, 1887, a cable arrived from Rome announcing McGlynn had been officially ex- communicated from the Church. For Catholics, there was no more severe a penalty than excommunication, and many who willingly had defied the hierarchy and had participated in Anti-Poverty Society meetings were now given pause. Risking the wrath of a pastor or archbishop was one thing; suffering the ultimate sanction in Church law—and thereby forfeiting any chance of eternal salvation—was quite another. In the bid for the allegiance of working-class Catholics between progressive labor activists and conservative church officials, the latter had just raised the stakes.[26]

Ultimately, that proved sufficient. While unprecedented in its size, scope, and duration, the organized defiance of clerical authority in support of McGlynn did not endure. After an initial outburst of indignation over McGlynn's excommunication, many supporters began to have second thoughts. The latter included journalist Patrick Ford. After nearly 20 years distinguishing himself as an outspoken advocate of radical social reform in Ireland and America, he openly broke with George and McGlynn for what he deemed their anticlericalism. Within weeks of the excommunication, quiet returned to St. Stephen's parish. So, too, did the contributions to the collection plate. The power of the Church proved to be too entrenched for anger over one priest's persecution to overcome it.

For the next five years, McGlynn worked on behalf of the poor through his Anti-Poverty Society. Eventually in 1892, the Vatican, without Archbishop Corrigan's prior knowledge, removed the order of excommunication. Forced to accept the return of his nemesis, Corrigan exiled McGlynn to St. Mary's parish in Newburgh, New York. He retained a devoted following at St. Stephen's, however, and returned there for special occasions to a warm reception. McGlynn died in Newburgh on January 7, 1900.[27]

The McGlynn affair ended in 1892, but it left a lasting imprint on the Catholic Church in New York and, to a degree, on the nation. At its core, it exposed the inadequacy of Catholic social teaching in the face of expansive laissez-faire industrial capitalism. Indeed, this revelation was so troubling that it prompted Pope Leo XIII to issue, in 1891, *Rerum Novarum* (*On the Condition of Labor*), an encyclical letter that supported moderate Catholic social reform and upheld the rights of Catholics to join labor unions. That document paved the way for the rise of progressive Catholics, most famously Father John A. Ryan (1865–1945), who explored the notion of a living wage in his dissertation, published in 1906.[28]

Change of a different and more tangible form, however, occurred on the ground. While few Catholics were prepared to embrace McGlynn's quasi-socialist radicalism, their support for the Land League, Henry George's ULP campaign, and McGlynn in his struggle with Corrigan indicated that they were searching for an effective alternative to the conservative, fatalist, offer-it-up approach to poverty and exploitation that had sustained them in the era of Archbishop John Hughes. That outlook, a product of virulent anti-Catholic nativism, traditional Irish peasant values, and Jansenist theology (a movement that emphasized original sin and human depravity), lost credibility in the Gilded Age. Diminished nativism (relatively speaking), greater assimilation, and upward mobility among Catholic immigrants in the 1880s—combined with intensified suffering and anxiety associated with industrialization—led New York Catholics to seek meaningful solutions. Ultimately, this new outlook found expression most concretely in the transformation not of the Church but rather of the one institution far more susceptible to the influence of everyday Catholics: Tammany Hall.

The divergent examples of two working-class Catholics will illustrate this point. In 1886, Thomas Flynn was an enthusiastic supporter of Henry George and McGlynn. When the latter was excommunicated, Flynn renounced his Catholic faith in protest. His daughter, Elizabeth Gurley Flynn, became one of the nation's most prominent radicals and head of the Communist Party in the United States. Yet despite her lifelong effort to bring about revolu-

24
The Standard, April 2 and May 7, 1887. See also Alfred Isacsson, *The Determined Doctor: The Story of Edward McGlynn* (Tarrytown, N.Y.: Vestigium Press, 1996), 162–166.

25
New York Herald, July 4, 1887.

26
New York Herald, July 4, 1887.

27
New York Herald, January 8, 1900, 1.

28
Mary Christine Athans, *Religion and Public Life: The Legacy of Monsignor John A. Ryan* (Lanham, Md.: University Press of America, 2001).

bring about revolutionary political, social, and economic change, she operated on the radical fringe of American life and ultimately exerted only a minimal influence.[29]

We find a far more representative response to the McGlynn affair in the experience of the Smith family. In 1886, Alfred E. Smith, Sr., stuck with Tammany Hall and voted a straight Democratic ticket. He died soon thereafter, a faithful Catholic to the end. In the same way that Elizabeth Gurley Flynn grew to embrace her father's radicalism and anticlericalism, Smith's son, Alfred, grew up devoted to the Catholic Church and the Democratic Party. Yet Smith's choices positioned him to become, beginning with his election to the State Assembly in 1903, the lead figure in the transformation of Tammany Hall from the conservative organization that turned a deaf ear to working-class demands in 1886 to a major agent of progressive social legislation. Indeed, Al Smith, the man who eventually became the first Catholic elected governor of New York and the first Catholic candidate for president nominated by a major party, emerged in the early 20th century as the face of an urban progressivism that sought to ameliorate the sufferings of the poor. Smith's career, therefore, reflected the inculcation of the broad vision, if not to the same radical degree, of liberal social policy espoused by Father Edward McGlynn in the city's Catholic culture.

29
Elizabeth Gurley Flynn, *The Rebel Girl: An Autobiography, My First Life, 1906–1926* (New York: International Publishers, 1973, orig. published as *I Speak My Own Piece: Autobiography of "The Rebel Girl,"* 1955), 43.

Dr. McGlynn at the unveiling of
a monument to Henry George,
Greenwood Cemetery, August 1898
Dr. McGlynn gave a funeral address for
George in 1897, and characterized him
as having "the heart of a hero."

JAMES T. FISHER

ON THE CATHOLIC WATERFRONT

STRUGGLING FOR POWER, OPPORTUNITY, AND JUSTICE

1

James Morris, *The Great Port: A Passage Through New York* (New York: Harcourt, Brace and World, 1969), 21; Russell Shorto, *The Island at the Center of the World: The Epic Story of Dutch Manhattan and the Forgotten Colony That Shaped America* (New York: Doubleday, 2004), 32.

The port made New York, and New York City Catholics made the port in the 19th century then ran it in the 20th.

New York is not the only city where Catholics found prominent places in politics, journalism, sports, and popular entertainment, but it is the one place where Catholic immigrants and their descendants built a port that made a global metropolis. The "commodious and delightful" harbor into which Henry Hudson piloted the Dutch East India Company vessel *Half Moon* in 1609 enjoyed abundant natural advantages over future rival ports, with a setting that was relatively free of ice and fog.[1] The port's human resources proved even more valuable when the port "took off" in the mid 19th century.

From the middle of the 19th century, as New York solidified its place as the nation's leading point of entry for goods and people, the Irish were the most conspicuous Catholics on its waterfront. While the early Irish community "contained many economic layers," including a fairly substantial pre-Famine cohort of skilled artisans both Catholic and Protestant, the great port was fueled by impoverished Irish Catholic refugees who sought work "in the least skilled, lowest paying jobs that New York City offered." Starting in the area along South Street, the Irish came to dominate the waterfront precincts along both shores of Lower Manhattan, working the maritime industries in every capacity, though predominately longshoring. "Irishmen took over New York's docks in the mid 19th century," wrote Edwin G. Burrows and Mike Wallace in *Gotham*:

On any given day five or six thousand of these "alongshoremen" moved mountains of cargo off ships and around the port, roaming from pier to pier for the "shape-ups" at which native-born stevedores amassed work crews. The work was hard, poorly paid, and erratic. While waiting for ships to arrive or weather to clear, men hung around local saloons, took alternate jobs as teamsters, boatmen, or brickmakers, and relied on the earnings of their wives and children.[2]

Stevedores hired men to load and unload ships. The work was exhausting and dangerous, and ethnic solidarity was the basis of the teamwork essential for survival. Irish longshoremen developed a proprietary attitude on the waterfront and viewed with suspicion African Americans and, later, immigrant workers from eastern and southern Europe whose shared Catholicism was trumped by Irish ethnic primacy. The earliest incarnations of longshoremen's unions were strictly local entities, rooted in ethnicity and neighborhood prerogatives, a pattern that endured in the port for more than a century. The city's horrific draft riots in July 1863 exploded in part from Irish dockworker resentment over the hiring of blacks as scab labor during a strike. Though most of the bloodshed occurred north of the most populated waterfront precincts, some Irish Americans seized the opportunity to declare "work upon the docks...shall be attended to solely by and absolutely by members of the 'Longshoremen's Association' and such white laborers as they see fit to permit upon the premises."[3]

A multiethnic New York Catholic waterfront was established in the late 19th and early 20th centuries out of a blend of business, political, and Church interests. Before Tammany Hall's William "Boss" Tweed was jailed in 1872, he ensured that the city's newly created Department of Docks reaped a "patronage windfall" for Tammany via contracts and licenses for a vast network of municipally owned piers constructed along Manhattan's Lower West Side. The collaboration between Tammany Hall and the New York Archdiocese was made evident not only by the marriage of "Honest John" Kelly—Tweed's immediate successor and Tammany's first Catholic boss—to the niece of New York archbishop John McCloskey, but also in the transformation of Manhattan's West Side from an Anglo-American stronghold into a Catholic mini-empire of several dozen old and new parishes. Priests routinely sent men to the piers bearing notes recommending them for employment; the parishes in turn were supported financially by self-made Catholic entrepreneurs whose dominance of waterfront industries was greatly enhanced by their Tammany connections.[4]

St. Veronica's in the West Village—established in 1887 just east of the Hudson riverbank, steps removed from busy Piers 45 and 46—and Sacred Heart parish on West 51st Street marked the geographic edges of Manhattan's western Catholic waterfront. The heart and soul of the area was Chelsea, the neighborhood between Greenwich Village and Hell's Kitchen. This waterfront "Vatican" was home to monumental pier facilities designed by the

2
Robert Greenhalgh Albion, *The Rise of New York Port, 1815–1860* (New York: Charles Scribner's Sons, 1939), 38–42; Donald Squires and Kevin Bone, "The Beautiful Lake: The Promise of the Natural Systems," in Kevin Bone, ed., *The New York Waterfront: Evolution and Building Culture of the Port of New York* (New York: Monacelli Press, 1997), 22, 26; Edwin G. Burrows and Mike Wallace, *Gotham: A History of New York City to 1898* (New York: Oxford University Press, 1999), 744.

3
David Montgomery, *The Fall of the House of Labor: The Workplace, the State, and American Labor Activism, 1865–1925* (Cambridge: Cambridge University Press, 1987), 96–99; Iver Bernstein, *The New York City Draft Riots: Their Significance for American Society and Politics in the Age of the Civil War* (New York: Oxford University Press, 1990), 27–28, 117–19; Calvin Winslow, "Introduction," *Waterfront Workers: New Perspectives on Race and Class* (Urbana: University of Illinois Press, 1998), 10.

4
For Tammany and the Department of Docks, see David Scobey, *Empire City: The Making and Meaning of the New York City Landscape* (Philadelphia: Temple University Press, 2002), 225–26.

TOP

On South Street New York—
Longshoremen Waiting For a Job, c. 1870,
wood engraving, from *Harper's Weekly*
The longshoreman at the right carries
a traditional cargo hook in his belt.

BOTTOM

Everett Shinn (1876–1953), *Near*
the New York Docks [Market
Scene], 1901, pastel

BOTTOM RIGHT

Scene on a New York Dock—Stevedores
Unloading, after a drawing by I. P.
Pranishnikoff, from *Harper's Weekly,*
July 14, 1877

TOP LEFT

Andrew Herman, *On the Waterfront*, 1940,
gelatin silver print.
Federal Art Project photographer Andrew
Herman captured dock workers at leisure.

TOP RIGHT

Berenice Abbott (1898–1991),
[Department of Docks Building, Pier A],
undated, gelatin silver print

BOTTOM

George Grantham Bain (1865–1944),
*New Chelsea Piers under construction,
New York*, 1909, gelatin silver print
The Chelsea Piers, Hudson River at 20th
Street, designed by Warren and Wetmore,
opened in 1910 after eight years of construction. The pink granite façades housing the passenger terminals for the White
Star and Cunard lines evoked a waterfront
cathedral. Chelsea Piers became a cargo
terminal in the late 1950s.

architectural firm Warren and Wetmore to rival in their splendor Grand Central Terminal—the firm's signature project—and erected between West 17th and West 23rd Streets during the first decade of the 20th century. The Chelsea Piers piersheds evoked a waterfront cathedral, in a neighborhood that housed not only the world's leading deep-sea shipping firms but also the port's dominant and most notorious labor union, the International Longshoremen's Association (ILA) whose "international" headquarters was located on West 14th Street in Chelsea. The ILA's seminal "Mother Local," Local 791, kept its offices at Twelfth Avenue and West 21st Street.[5]

From this foundation a New York Catholic waterfront ethos emerged in the years just prior to World War I, marked by an intense disdain for outsiders and a self-regulating social order in which violent internal conflicts were covered by a daunting code of silence that prevailed from Greenwich Village to Hell's Kitchen. The waterfront's ethnic hierarchy mirrored that of its host archdiocese, with a wholly Irish top leadership ruling over an increasingly diverse constituency. Over 90 percent of the ILA's membership in the port was Catholic, with Italians supplanting the Irish as the largest dockworker community early in the 20th century. Italian Americans soon dominated the vast South Brooklyn waterfront and the smaller shipping operations on Staten Island. There were also substantial communities of Polish and Yugoslavian longshoremen in the port, generically mislabeled by the Irish as "Austrians."

The port's ethnic diversity created opportunities for Italians and a few Poles to dominate some ILA locals. Their control of hiring on neighborhood piers in Brooklyn, Staten Island, and parts of Hudson County generated sufficient economic and political power to cause the central ILA's leadership periodic discomfort. The port's largest predominantly non-Catholic dockworker group, Local 968, made up of African Americans, remained strictly beholden to white-ethnic hiring bosses and was hindered by its inability to control any piers. Ultimately, control of the union at the highest level remained in the hands of Irish-Americans with close ties to the New York Archdiocese. Joseph P. Ryan, a Chelsea product who ascended to the union's presidency in 1927 and was anointed "life-president" in 1943, lived across Tenth Avenue from Guardian Angel parish, the "Shrine Church of the Sea," whose beautiful Romanesque church—replacing an earlier incarnation—opened in 1930 on West 22nd Street. Guardian Angel's pastor after 1934 was Monsignor John J. O'Donnell, the port chaplain and an ardently outspoken champion of Ryan and the Catholic waterfront entrepreneurs who employed Ryan's union membership. Msgr. O'Donnell was a de facto bishop of the port; historian Bruce Nelson has described him as "Cardinal [Francis] Spellman's official representative on the waterfront."[6]

The Irish gradually lost control of virtually all the working piers in the port, which also encompassed the densely populated waterfront of Hudson County, New Jersey, but Catho-

5
For the establishment of St. Veronica's, see Thomas J. Shelley, *Greenwich Village Catholics: St. Joseph's Church and the Evolution of an Urban Faith Community, 1829–2002* (Washington, D.C.: Catholic University of America Press, 2003), 101–2, 105–8; and Henry J. Browne, *One Stop Above Hell's Kitchen: Sacred Heart Parish in Clinton* (South Hackensack, N.J.: CustomBook, 1977), 29, 69. For the Chelsea Piers, see Mary Beth Betts, "Masterplanning: Municipal Support of Maritime Transport and Commerce 1870-1930s," in Bone, *New York Waterfront*, 42–44, 69–70.

6
Bruce Nelson, *Divided We Stand: American Workers and the Struggle for Black Equality* (Princeton, N.J.: Princeton University Press, 2001), 77–78.

lics did not. As miniature ethnic enclaves, these piers resembled the "national" parishes established in the late 19th and early 20th centuries. Pier hiring bosses of various ethnic backgrounds, who chose longshoremen for shift work either by the "shape-up" system or as members of regular work gangs, were linked to the West Side Irish rulers of the ILA in a manner akin to that of Italian or Polish pastors beholden to Irish-American bishops who attempted to orchestrate the religious politics of ethnic succession. The Irish leaders of Tammany Hall pursued a similar strategy. But ethnic succession unfolded *first* in the port, in a fashion that presaged seismic shifts in the Church and the city's political machines.

Catholic control of the piers was but one element in a developing New York waterfront hierarchy that saw self-made entrepreneurs such as Michael Moran—whose purchase of a single towboat in 1860 laid the foundation for the world's largest tugboat fleet—and William J. McCormack achieve extraordinary wealth, political influence, and spiritual authority. McCormack was born in the West Village in 1887. His father was an impoverished wagon driver who, after losing his job, moved his family across the Hudson River to Jersey City. Bill McCormack's rapid ascent from teamster to bistate tycoon was grounded in the political connections he cultivated on both sides of the river, with both the Hague machine in Hudson County and West Side Tammany chieftains. After establishing himself in the brutally competitive stevedoring business on the Lower West Side during World War I, McCormack helped organize a large trucking firm, the board of which was chaired by Alfred E. Smith after he lost reelection to the governorship in 1920. McCormack parlayed such connections into the greatest entrepreneurial coup in the history of the Port in 1930, when he secured the contract to handle the stevedoring for all of the Pennsylvania Railroad's freight operations on its six West Side piers. Three years later, he acquired the rights to stevedore the Pennsylvania's freight in the enormous Jersey City rail terminal. Since there was no rail tunnel to connect the American mainland and New York City, Bill McCormack gained enormous power with his influence in the network of waterborne commerce that moved goods from one side of the Hudson to the other. As an unidentified longshoreman explained to an investigator around 1950, "to get to any market in the city, it had to come through McCormack.... [W]hoever planned this whole thing out was plannin' that you and I and anybody else would stop eatin' if they said so."[7]

Bill McCormack controlled the unions representing his employees, including the ILA—a practice that was viewed on the New York waterfront as a sign of his legitimacy. "King Joe" Ryan reigned over the ILA at McCormack's pleasure and maintained cordial relationships with shippers and stevedoring firms. As a result, there were no officially sanctioned strikes in the port between 1919 and 1948.

Church officials reinforced this model of class harmony and social order along the piers. An exceedingly prominent figure in the New York Archdiocese and a generous benefactor,

[7] Bill McCormack may be the most important historical figure in New York City to remain almost completely unknown, to scholars and the general public alike. His career as "Mr. Big" is treated in detail in my forthcoming study, *The Irish Waterfront and the Soul of the Port: New York/New Jersey, 1917–1954*. Most of the material cited in this essay is drawn from that study. The unidentified informant is quoted in "Transcript of an Interview with a Longshoreman," n.d., 8, Box 11, folder 4, Xavier Institute of Industrial Relations Papers, O'Hare Special Collections, Walsh Library, Fordham University, New York.

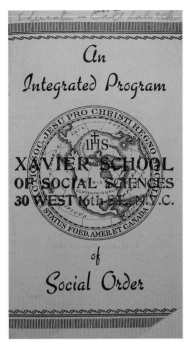

TOP LEFT

An Integrated Program of Social Order
[overstamped Xavier School of Social
Sciences, 30 West 16th Street, N.Y.C.],
pamphlet

The Xavier Labor School, founded in 1936,
was part of a network of Jesuit-sponsored
labor schools within New York City.

TOP CENTER

Rev. William J. Smith, S.J., *The Catholic
Labor School: Common Sense in Action*
(New York, 1941)

This pamphlet outlined the message of
Christian social reconstruction offered
to workers.

TOP RIGHT

Emblem of the International Longshoremen's Association (ILA), c. 1901

Founded by Great Lakes maritime workers,
the ILA arrived on the New York City
waterfront with ILA Local 791 in May 1908.

BOTTOM

Longshoremen vote at a meeting of the
ILA, October 14, 1945

This meeting took place at Manhattan
Centre, after two weeks of an unsanc-
tioned strike. The strike broke on its 18th
day, when more than 10,000 workers
returned to the docks.

McCormack was honored with papal appointments ranging from Grand Knight of the Holy Sepulchre to Knight of the Grand Cross to membership in the Knights of Malta. Mc-Cormack staunchly upheld a waterfront social order that appeared to many on the outside as brutal, lawless, and uncivilized. He projected an intimacy with violence that featured spiritual overtones; only those who had fought their way to the top were authorized to mediate waterfront life. Dozens and possibly scores of longshoremen disappeared along the West Side between 1920 and 1950 with murder the most common cause: some men were killed in random bar fights and tossed in the river; others—it is impossible to determine how many—were victims of pier-related violence, with disputes over control of hiring and public loading on individual piers the most frequent trigger. The Church pursued a militantly hands-off policy toward waterfront violence, a position continually reinforced from the pulpit by Monsignor O'Donnell, who repeatedly said that his parishioner Joe Ryan "keeps his hands off the spiritual things of my church and I keep my hands out of his business."[8]

This waterfront regime did not go unchallenged within the Church, but the reform efforts in the 1930s of the Catholic Worker movement and its offshoot, the Association of Catholic Trade Unionists, were easily dismissed as the work of radicals. The emergence in the late 1940s of a waterfront apostolate conducted out of the Xavier Labor School on West 16th Street in Chelsea by a young Jesuit, John M. Corridan, signaled a potent new force that changed the shape of the Catholic waterfront. Founded in 1936, the Xavier Labor School was part of a growing network of Jesuit-sponsored such schools (in addition to those operated by dioceses), designed to prevent communist takeover of unions by offering workers a positive message of Christian social reconstruction.

Inspired by the Church's social encyclicals, Corridan and his more cautious but equally dedicated supervisor, Philip Carey, S.J., made the Xavier Labor School the focal point of a campaign for union democracy and waterfront social justice. Widely viewed as outsiders with connections to Anglo-Republican politicians and reformers they largely failed to inspire a grassroots insurgency among the men, but Corridan succeeded spectacularly in assembling a coalition of largely non-Catholic journalists, reformers, and filmmakers who shared his passion. Beginning with an autumn 1948 series of *New York Sun* articles by investigative journalist Malcolm Johnson—for which Corridan served as key source, and for which Johnson won a Pulitzer Prize—the Jesuits sparked extraordinary interest from beyond the waterfront, resulting in sensational public hearings conducted by the New York State Crime Commission in the fall and winter of 1952–1953, which confirmed Johnson/Corridan's depiction of the Port of New York as a "jungle, an outlaw frontier."[9]

Corridan's most enduring ally was the novelist and screenwriter Budd Schulberg, who, while not a Catholic, became the most effective and theologically literate "mouthpiece," as he put it, for Corridan and his very small band of "rebel disciples." In addition to writing

8
Msgr. O'Donnell was quoted in the *New York World-Telegram and Sun*, April 27, 1953.
9
The Pulitzer Prize-winning "Crime on the Waterfront" series is reprinted in Malcolm Johnson, *On The Waterfront* (New York: Chamberlain Bros., 2005).

stirring essays about the West Side waterfront that were published in *The New York Times Magazine* in the early 1950s, Schulberg worked for nearly four years on a screenplay inspired by Johnson's investigations, Corridan's analysis of waterfront crime—especially the "shape-up" system of hiring—and a shared vision of waterfront redemption through personal witness to truth. It took four years for the film *On the Waterfront* to surmount political and movie-industry obstacles before it was finally produced on the streets and piers of Hoboken, New Jersey, in late autumn and early winter of 1953–1954. *On the Waterfront* benefited greatly from enthusiastic behind-the-scenes support from Austin J. Tobin, the executive director of the Port of New York Authority since 1942. The grandson of a Brooklyn Irish longshore-man who died in an accident at age 30, Tobin ranked alongside his even more publicity-shy nemesis Bill McCormack as the most powerful figure in the port. When McCormack was finally "exposed" as the port's "Mr. Big" during the 1952 state Crime Commission hearings, he sought to have himself dubbed "the Little Man's Port Authority" instead.[10]

When *On the Waterfront's* creators pleaded with Tobin for help in securing a pier on which to shoot key scenes, he forced a stevedoring firm—newly indicted in the wake of the state Crime Commission hearings—to relinquish control of Hoboken's Pier 1 for "renovations" (the pier was later modernized and rechristened Pier C). Tobin shared Corridan's horror over waterfront violence and criminality. He emerged from the shadows in 1953 to join the Jesuits' campaign on behalf of a Bi-State Waterfront Commission that would register long-shoremen and police the piers while enabling the Port Authority to expand its entrepreneur-ial ambitions throughout New York Harbor. Working together, Corridan and Tobin helped reshape the moral and physical contours of the great port, paying tribute in the process to the generations of immigrants that had begun their American sojourns in New York Harbor. They honored especially those who had remained in the port to toil and suffer under its often brutal conditions. "What confronts us along Twelfth Avenue and West Street," Tobin said in lauding Corridan in 1953:

> is not a material problem but a moral problem. It calls for civic confession, penance
> and reform and not for phony explanations. That's the reason the waterfront gospel
> of Father John M. Corridan preached with all the courage of his soldierly progenitor,
> Francis Xavier, goes right to the heart of our waterfront problem.[11]

Yet while the Waterfront Commission went into operation in December 1953—and *On the Waterfront* won eight Academy Awards in 1954, including Best Picture, Best Actor (Marlon Brando as longshoreman Terry Malloy), and Best Story and Screenplay—waterfront reform-ers were unable to oust the ILA from its power base in the port. In two successive elections (December 1953 and May 1954), the union was narrowly recertified by votes of the rank and file. Despite the ouster and subsequent indictment of Joe Ryan in 1953 and the expul-sion of the union from the American Federation of Labor that same year, the ILA remained

10
For Austin J. Tobin and the Port Authority, see Jameson W. Doig, *Empire on the Hud-son: Entrepreneurial Vision and Political Power at the Port of New York and New Jersey* (New York: Columbia University Press, 2001).

11
Austin J. Tobin is quoted in a letter from Philip A. Carey, S.J., to Dennis J. Comey, S.J., March 11, 1953, Xavier Labor School, folder 1, Archives of the New York Jesuit Province, New York.

ensconced in the port and mired in links to organized-crime families, even as the water-front labor market was forever altered by the introduction of container-ship technology in the 1960s. Containerization required far fewer but better-skilled longshoremen: the vastly increased size of container ships and access to intermodal transfers (from ships to trucks and rail) resulted in a shift in the port's center of gravity from the West Side of Manhattan to the Ports of Newark and Elizabeth in New Jersey. New York chauvinists insisted on viewing Newark and Elizabeth as remote outposts, although these facilities were well within the historic boundaries of the Port and they sustained the traditions of the Catholic waterfront—the Archdiocese of Newark had a fulltime chaplain on the piers for many years.[12]

The Port Authority orchestrated the development of Ports Newark and Elizabeth, but the crowning achievement of Austin Tobin's long tenure at the bi-state agency was the planning and construction of the World Trade Center in the 1960s. This gargantuan feat was undertaken in partnership with banker/civic leader David Rockefeller, whose brother Nelson was the governor of New York State. The massive, imposing trade center—with its initial focus on global maritime commerce—both fulfilled and complicated the legacy of the Catholic waterfront. It confirmed the stature of Tobin—the Brooklyn longshoremen's grandson—as dominant architect of the port's political economy even as it undermined, in its vast impersonal character, the local communal traditions that had graced (and sometimes plagued) the port from its inception. Over time, the trade center's harsher features were softened by familiarity and even affection, as it became the port's most recognizable landmark. In the terrible aftermath of the attacks that destroyed the trade center on September 11, 2001, observers from other parts of the country and the world were moved by the profoundly communal character of the local response to the tragedy. The deep roots of many victims in the neighborhoods of the historic Catholic waterfront—though many now lived elsewhere—were frequently noted in tributes. The New York Catholic waterfront's legacy is complex, its history often marked by internal strife, but its role in shaping the intimately local dimensions of the world's greatest metropolis remains vividly evident.[13]

12
For containerization, see Marc Levinson, *The Box: How the Shipping Container Made the World Smaller and the World Economy Bigger* (Princeton, N.J.: Princeton University Press, 2006), 21.

13
For Tobin and the World Trade Center, see Angus Kress Gillespie, *Twin Towers: The Life of New York City's World Trade Center* (New Brunswick, N.J.: Rutgers University Press, 1999); James Glanz and Eric Lipton, *City in the Sky: The Rise and Fall of the World Trade Center* (New York: Times Books, 2003).

Film still of Marlon Brando and Eva
Marie Saint in *On the Waterfront*, 1954
Brando won an Academy Award for his
role as longshoreman Terry Malloy in
the movie based on the waterfront
apostolate conducted by Jesuit
John M. Corridan.

AN AFTERWORD: THE NEW CATHOLIC NEW YORK

William Donohue with a graduating
student from St. Lucy's, 1976

WILLIAM A. DONOHUE

Spanish Harlem Welcomes an Irishman

The year was 1973, and I was looking for a job as a teacher. My only guide was the telephone books for Manhattan, Queens, and the Bronx, where I took note of 59 Catholic schools. I wrote to every one of them, asking for a job. I wrote to schools named after saints I revered as well as those I had never heard of. Before long, one of the saints got back to me: St. Lucy. The principal of St. Lucy's, an Irishman, said he was ready to offer me the job, but the pastor, an Italian, interrupted the conversation and said they would have to get back to me.

The next day the principal called again and formally extended an offer, confessing that there really was no competition. That's because the school was located on East 104th Street in Spanish Harlem—a poor neighborhood that suffered from crime and other ailments.

Not too many teachers wanted to work there, but for me, the location was a plus. I had been trained as an accountant while in the U.S. Air Force and was offered several accounting jobs after I finished college, but my heart wasn't in it. For someone who was doing graduate work in sociology at the time, St. Lucy's was a godsend—a veritable laboratory for any student of the subject.

The initial reaction of the neighborhood's Puerto Ricans and African Americans to a new white man was chilly. In El Barrio, white people tended to be either doctors, teachers, or drug pushers. But once the third graders ran to hold my hand while crossing the street, the locals got to know that I was a teacher and that I was not the enemy. Indeed, it didn't take long before they embraced me. It was a reciprocal relationship.

Never in my life have I met more generous people than those who lived in Spanish Harlem. At Christmastime, I would walk down 104th Street (the school was located between First and Second Avenues—it has since closed because of declining enrollment) with shopping bags full of gifts on both arms. It made no difference what grade I taught. I started as homeroom teacher in the third grade, then moved to the seventh and eighth grades—the reception was the same. But it would be dishonest to say there weren't any problems.

Most of the teachers were women, and since I was the big Irishman, it fell to me to search the school when a stranger wandered in off the street. There were gangs that had to be dealt with, and that meant escorting students home for fear of attack. Then there was the man with the mirrored eyeglasses—you couldn't see his eyes, just your own reflection.

The eighth grade girls were a tough bunch, but the man with the mirrored eyeglasses unnerved them. He never touched them—though he came brazenly close—preferring to shadow them while making sexual remarks. Then, on the very day the students threw a party for me after I passed my Ph.D. oral exam, I noticed a man outside during lunch break who looked downright creepy. He walked up to some of the women teachers on the sidewalk and began staring at them, standing only inches away. As I approached him, some of the eighth grade girls on their way home to lunch screamed that this was the same guy—the guy with the mirror glasses—who had been harassing them. He immediately walked briskly down the street.

That was it. Pumped up by the party, and bolstered by a rush of adrenalin, I took after him. The students—there must have been a hundred of them—came charging down the street screaming for me to get him. It was like the scene in Rocky where all the kids followed the champ. No matter how many times I told them to back off, they followed me nonetheless. On the corner was Wayne, a cop whom I had befriended. He offered his assistance but I waved him off.

Then I caught up with him. Yes, it was the man with the mirrored eyeglasses. I pushed him up against a fence, grabbed his hands (lest he reach for a blade or gun) and issued a warning that was unmistakable. He didn't flinch. Nor did he ever bother my students again.

It was a great feeling for an Irishman to be welcomed in a neighborhood like Spanish Harlem. Whether playing basketball on weekends with the older kids, or taking 50 or 60 students to Yankee Stadium or Shea Stadium on a Saturday, it was nothing but gratifying. It also impressed upon me the stupidity of prejudice.

Prejudice is more than wrong—it is stupid. It is stupid because there is so much joy to be had when all of God's children can party together. Fortunately, shutting people out is not the Catholic way, and in this

regard I was blessed to have the opportunity to teach religion and social studies, subjects that lent themselves to discussions on the richness of the human experience and the inherent dignity that we all possess.

If my students succeeded in learning this lesson—and I think most did—then it was worth the effort. It most assuredly was what made St. Lucy's different from the public school directly across the street. The school had to be closed because of violent incidents.

There is a ton of empirical evidence demonstrating the unheralded success of Catholic schools in the inner city. They succeed because they offer structure where there is little, discipline where it is uncommon, and a sense of community where it is lacking. And they provide students with a teleology, one that is grounded in faith.

It is fashionable today to cast religion as the enemy of freedom. It is anything but. My students at St. Lucy's were able to grow in freedom precisely because they were nurtured in the soil of restraint and the love of God. And they awakened in me as well a renewed interest in Catholicism. It is simply not possible to teach religion honestly and not rethink your own faith.

It is for these reasons that I chalk up my experience in Spanish Harlem as a learning experience for everyone involved. Moreover, when Puerto Rican and African-American students meshed with their Irish-American teacher in New York in the early 1970s, it certainly was a sign that someone is directing traffic from above.

DAVID A. BADILLO

A NEW MISSION

CARDINAL SPELLMAN AND NEW YORK'S PUERTO RICANS

For the urban historian, as for religious scholars, the work of Cardinal Francis Spellman (1889–1967) has been uniquely significant. He was the most influential of a network of U.S. prelates that rose to power in the 1940s—including Archbishop Robert Lucey of San Antonio and Cardinal Samuel Stritch of Chicago, each with large metropolitan constituencies of Latinos. Spellman keenly observed changing neighborhoods and chronicled these and other urban patterns closely, often working with powerful politicians to reshape local infrastructures. He was, of course, also a national—indeed international   player, negotiating with bishops in Puerto Rico on matters of religion and politics while participating in the periodic meetings of the Bishops' Committee for the Spanish-Speaking, which among its many efforts, sought to provide visiting Mexican priests to communities of immigrant farm workers in the Southwest and Midwest. His early support of the phasing out of the national parish concept in favor of geographically based parishes revealed him as an ardent "Americanizer." Yet his support of bilingual and bicultural training for a generation of postwar seminarians at the Catholic University in Puerto Rico (and their subsequent placement in the barrios of New York City) helped narrow communication gaps that had long existed between Catholic clergy and Latino parishioners in the New York Archdiocese.

Spellman was archbishop of New York from 1939 until his death, a span which saw huge cultural, economic, and physical changes in the city, especially after World War II. During much of the 1950s, master builder Robert Moses laid the basis for moving existing slums and creating new ones, constructing 24 public housing projects and 11 superhighways throughout the city. Those projects disrupted entire neighborhoods and led to dramatic changes in Catholic New York. Older Latino neighborhoods, such as those in South Brooklyn and Red Hook, declined after highway construction around the Brooklyn Navy Yard and Brooklyn Civic Center. The construction of the Cross-Bronx Expressway in the late 1950s ignored established neighborhood patterns and drove out thousands of middle-class Jewish and Italian residents. Wholesale displacement of Puerto Ricans and blacks from Manhattan's Upper West Side was justified as providing an opportunity to create "balanced communities" in the outer boroughs. Municipal officials' approval of these processes exacerbated racial tensions and encouraged "white flight."[1]

In the 1940s and 1950s, and even beyond, East Harlem's La Milagrosa parish remained central to Puerto Rican Catholic life in New York, with parishioners coming not only from all over El Barrio but from other neighborhoods and even from the Bronx, in spite of the fact that their territorial parishes were by then also offering services in Spanish. In one parish that quickly turned Puerto Rican in Manhattan's Upper West Side in the 1950s, St. Rose of Lima church in Washington Heights, rural Puerto Rican migrants practiced Catholicism largely without a clergy, organizing confraternities and providing catechetical instruction.

Soon groups of lay catechists formed, including the *Hijas de Maria* (Daughters of Mary) and *la Sociedad del Santo Nombre* (Holy Name Society), marking the emergence of an impromptu parish community. Finally parishioners approached the church's Irish-American pastor and requested a Spanish-speaking priest to celebrate Mass so that they would not have to travel to one of the existing Spanish-language chapels. The pastor invited a religious order priest from Spain to provide first a monthly Mass and then a "basement service."[2]

Cardinal Spellman played a key role in the development of ministry to Puerto Ricans, financing personnel, institutional changes, and other changes, but the archdiocese also recognized the role of all ethnicities in city building. By the early 20th century, Italian Americans, who had arrived several generations earlier, had gained control over many of East Harlem's neighborhood institutions. The Church of Mount Carmel on 115th Street was transformed increasingly into an Italian-American parish during the 1940s and 1950s. It remained inaccessible and impenetrable to Puerto Rican newcomers, though both groups were predominantly Catholic. Puerto Ricans' and Italians' frequent conflicts with each other, however, mirrored the Italians' experience with other ethnic groups and the archdiocese.[3]

In the 1950s, when Catholic office seekers still depended on the Church's political contacts to obtain votes and jobs, the archdiocese became an institutional power partly because of the educational, hospital and charity services it provided. Spellman retained clout in other secular processes and institutions throughout his tenure, as was seen in 1955, when

1
Robert A. Caro, *The Powerbroker: Robert Moses and the Fall of New York* (New York: Vintage Books, 1974), 740, 741, 845.
2
Ana Maria Diaz-Stevens, *Oxcart Catholicism on Fifth Avenue: The Impact of the Puerto Rican Migration upon the Archdiocese of New York* (Notre Dame, Ind.: University of Notre Dame Press, 1993), 112.
3
Robert A. Orsi, *The Madonna on 115th Street: Faith and Community in Italian Harlem, 1880–1950* (New Haven, Conn.: Yale University Press, 1985), 102, 182, 183.

TOP
Harry J. Fields, [Cardinal Francis Spellman performing a ceremony], 1950s
Cardinal Spellman created the Office of Spanish Catholic Action of the Archdiocese of New York in March 1953 to coordinate Puerto Rican ministry.

BOTTOM
H. Armstrong Roberts, [Spanish Harlem street scene], 1960s
After World War II, the Spanish-speaking population of New York City, mostly Puerto Rican, grew rapidly, with many settling in East Harlem's *El Barrio* neighborhood.

the Jesuit-led Fordham University wanted to open a campus in midtown Manhattan. That brought Moses into the picture. He used his sweeping powers as Slum Clearance Committee chair and city construction coordinator to oust hundreds of tenants from six prime acres of real estate adjacent to his Lincoln Center Title I development. Many of the displaced residents at the location where the Fordham campus was placed were themselves Catholic, including Irish Americans and Puerto Ricans. St. Matthew's parish on West 68th Street, deemed expendable, was destroyed in the course of renewal.

Spellman desegregated his archdiocese's charitable and educational institutions and played an important role as emissary between the White House and New York. He also became involved with Latin American issues. By 1940, six Roman Catholic churches served Puerto Ricans and other Spanish speakers almost exclusively, with at least two others having a Spanish Mass. No new national parishes—for whose founding or discontinuance permission from the Vatican would have been required—were established. The new model of an "integrated" or mixed parish became the accepted method for meeting the needs of Puerto Ricans and, later, other Latinos. Many integrated parishes developed out of informal agreements between neighboring pastors, often without the archbishop's involvement, allowing Spanish-speaking residents to receive the sacraments.[4]

Spellman saw national parishes as reinforcing ethnic identity even to the point of segregation, as had occurred with African Americans, and feared that setting up national parishes for Puerto Ricans would retard their assimilation. In New York, Puerto Ricans were scattered among numerous neighborhoods, many of which were disrupted by the construction of vast low-income high-rise housing projects, as well as urban renewal programs. It became more difficult for Puerto Ricans to create cohesive communities within neighborhoods than it had been for earlier immigrant groups. As they entered new areas, they became minorities in territorial parishes. The Spanish Mass allowed them a minimum of sacred space, though at the cost of keeping them apart from English-speaking parishioners. In practice, Puerto Ricans proved very reluctant to give up their rural customs or abandon their religious practices, and Spellman respected this. But he sought to modify the popular religious practices of Puerto Ricans to increasingly center them on receiving the Mass and sacraments.

In March 1953, Spellman created the Office of Spanish Catholic Action of the Archdiocese of New York to coordinate Puerto Rican ministry. It was headed by Monsignor Joseph F. Connolly, a respected priest. Within a few weeks of his appointment, Connolly began the institution of the Fiesta of St. John the Baptist—the island's patron saint—as a focus for Puerto Rican Catholic identity. To varying degrees, the archdiocese used the fiesta to foster a sense of unity between Puerto Ricans and other Spanish-speaking Catholics, and ultimately between them and all Catholics in New York. In 1953, the fiesta included a pontifical Mass

4
Jaime R. Vidal, "Popular Religion among the Hispanics in the General Area of Newark." In *Presencia Nueva, Knowledge for Service and Hope: A Study of Hispanics in the Archdiocese of Newark.* Edited by the Archdiocese of Newark (Newark, N.J.: Archdiocese of Newark, 1988), 72.

at St. Patrick's Cathedral, celebrated by Bishop James McManus of Ponce, with Spellman presiding and the mayor of New York and a number of other civic leaders present.[5]

In 1957 Connolly's successor, Father James J. Wilson, rented Randall's Island stadium and park, a location easily accessible from Manhattan's Lower East Side. For the next eight years this remained the fiesta's location. The event featured a procession of lay sodalities and confraternities, who marched behind their respective banners, followed by an outdoor Mass with a Spanish sermon given by a guest preacher and concluding remarks by the cardinal. An accompanying civic ceremony brought the participation of local and island politicians and leaders, which culminated with the awarding of that year's San Juan Medal. There was also a cultural celebration featuring Puerto Rican music, theater, and other forms of entertainment. By the late 1950s, annual attendance at the fiesta averaged more than 55,000.[6]

The early 1950s also saw the beginning of another of Spellman's initiatives, this one involving sending a number of priests and seminarians to Puerto Rico to learn the language and culture of the island; this proved to be useful and practical training for work in New York's parishes. In view of the general shortage of priests on the island, it was generally agreed that a Puerto Rican priest was needed more on the island than he would be needed on the continent. Several priests and seminarians went to Puerto Rico each year from 1953 to 1955; in 1956 and 1957 the cardinal accelerated the process, sending half of his ordination class for special Spanish-language training, first at Georgetown University and then to Puerto Rico. Under the influence of young priest Ivan Illich, the archdiocese embarked on a vision of integrating Puerto Ricans with priests who were not only bilingual but bicultural and versed in the migrants' religious tradition. Father Illich, only in his late twenties, was temporarily assigned to Ponce to develop an extensive training program at the Catholic University, which was financially underwritten by Spellman and geared to training priests for the Archdiocese of New York. In 1959 it took the name Institute of Intercultural Communication; it remained active until 1972.[7]

Many of the younger priests, sisters, brothers, and laypeople trained at the institute became pastors, teachers, and important advocates in ministry to Puerto Ricans. Though under Spellman's control, the institute also contributed to other continental dioceses' ministries for Puerto Ricans and other immigrants from Latin America. The continued post-war influx prompted the New York Archdiocese and the Brooklyn Diocese to begin registering people for mainland parishes even before they left Puerto Rico. The existing Vincentian and Augustinian parishes in Manhattan (Esperanza and Our Lady of Guadalupe) were staffed by priests from the continental United States, Spain, and a few other European countries, and many of them had never gone to Puerto Rico. Meanwhile, a large number of the Brooklyn clergy came from Spain. There were very few Puerto Rican priests. Several congregations of nuns from the Brooklyn Diocese, who had gone into Puerto Rico early in the 20th century, continued to render valuable assistance in schools. They directed boarding houses for

5
Jaime R. Vidal, "Citizens Yet Strangers: The Puerto Rican Experience." In *Puerto Rican and Cuban Catholics in the U.S., 1900–1965*. Edited by Jay P. Dolan and Jaime R. Vidal (Notre Dame, Ind.: University of Notre Dame Press, 1994), 94.

6
Ibid., 101.

7
Joseph P. Fitzpatrick, *The Stranger Is Our Own: Reflections on the Journey of Puerto Rican Migrants* (Kansas City, Mo.: Sheed and Ward, 1996).

young women and expanded catechetical work among public school children, while assisting the Redemptorists and other religious orders.[8]

The Spanish Vincentians actively ministered to the needs of many of Brooklyn's Puerto Ricans, while a number of diocesan priests from the Brooklyn Diocese began to study Spanish on their own. In 1958 Bishop Bryan J. McEntegart began assigning newly ordained priests to study Spanish at the Catholic University of Ponce in Puerto Rico, which would also offer an opportunity for cultural immersion. Puerto Rico's religious order clergy— led by the predominately U.S. Redemptorists, who clustered in larger Puerto Rican cities and towns—outnumbered diocesan priests by more than three to one. By 1960 some two hundred diocesan priests had been trained, and within a decade nearly three hundred additional priests, religious and laypeople had studied in Ponce's Institute of Intercultural Communication.[9]

In 1961, there were 42 Catholic parishes in New York City with Spanish-speaking Roman Catholic priests, but only one was Puerto Rican. By contrast, preachers and ministers of Pentecostal churches in New York were almost all Puerto Ricans, which meant that in such churches members could rise rapidly. Pentecostals had been looked upon as most heretical by the more mainline or "ecumenical" Protestant denominations. In Puerto Rico, Pentecostals were not in on the original division of the Protestant pie, and thus they could form congregations anywhere on the island. Protestant leaders of all stripes perceived widespread religious indifference among Puerto Ricans in New York City. Estimates identified almost half of the total New York City population in 1952 as Roman Catholic, but only about one-third were actually affiliated with the Catholic Church. Among Puerto Ricans the figure was much lower, and fully 50 percent of their marriages were being conducted in Protestant churches.[10]

By 1965, Puerto Ricans were further removed from the pan-Latino identity of neighborhoods in the 1920s and 1930s, when they had shared streets and parishes with Cubans, Spaniards, and Latin Americans as part of a larger Spanish-speaking community. The massive migration of the mid 1940s through the mid 1960s had no contemporary counterparts other than the northern migration of southern blacks; the groups competed for jobs, residence, and economic standing. The Puerto Rican color line became increasingly confusing and frustrating; reluctant ethnics, they were ambivalent about their perceived standing as nonwhite racial minorities. Puerto Ricans in New York City passively resisted Americanization, however, holding on to their language and culture rather than integrating into parish communities.[11]

Language and identity, of course, are hardly new issues for the Catholic Church in New York. The city's Latinos not only have transformed the city, they have returned the Church to its immigrant roots.

8
Robert I. Gannon, *Up to the Present: The Story of Fordham* (Garden City, N.Y.: Doubleday, 1967), 272; John Cooney, *The American Pope: The Life and Times of Francis Cardinal Spellman* (New York: Times Books, 1984), 323.

9
Diocese of Brooklyn, *Diocese of Immigrants: The Brooklyn Catholic Experience, 1853–2003* (Strasbourg, France: Editions du Signe, 2004), 122.

10
Nathan Glazer and Daniel P. Moynihan, *Beyond the Melting Pot: The Negroes, Puerto Ricans, Jews, Italians, and Irish of New York City* 2nd ed. (Cambridge, Mass,: Massachusetts Institute of Technology Press, 1970), 106; Dan Wakefield, *Island in the City: The World of Spanish Harlem* (Boston: Houghton Mifflin, 1959), 62, 65, 76.

11
See Rosa Estades, "Symbolic Unity: The Puerto Rican Day Parade." In *The Puerto Rican Struggle: Essays on Survival in the U.S.* Edited by Clara E. Rodriguez, Virginia Sanchez Korrol, and Jose Oscar Alers (New York: Puerto Rican Migration Research Consortium, 1980) and Nathan Kantrowitz, *Ethnic and Racial Segregation in the New York Metropolis: Residential Patterns among White Ethnic Groups, Blacks, and Puerto Ricans* (New York: Praeger, 1973).

TOP

La Fiesta de San Juan Bautista, Randall's
Island, June 7, 1962
Celebration of the *San Juan Fiesta,* Puerto
Rico's patron saint, began in 1953. In 1957,
the fiesta moved to Randall's Island, with
a procession, outdoor Mass, and concluding
remarks by Cardinal Spellman.

BOTTOM

Dignitaries marching in *La Fiesta de
San Juan Bautista* procession, Randall's
Island, June 7, 1962
Among the invited political figures
pictured are Antonio Mendez, the first
native-born Puerto Rican to be named a
Democratic Party district leader in New
York; Manhattan Borough President
Hulan Jack; Felipe N. Torres, the first
Puerto Rican elected to the New
York State Assembly from the Bronx;
and Doña Felisa Rincon de Gaultier,
the flamboyant mayor of San Juan,
Puerto Rico, whose presence marked
the celebration as unmistakably
Puerto Rican.

GREEN GRASS, CAPE CODS, AND SUBURBAN CATHOLICISM

Set your mind's clock to that time after a president's assassination in Dallas but before an astronaut's stroll on the Moon; after a New York City World's Fair but before a New York Mets World Series. A boy with a concave chest and a considerable overbite emerges from a house that looks like every other house on his block and squints into the morning light.

Standing there, frozen in fear, he could be mistaken for a new lawn ornament, another desperate reach for neighborhood distinction by those crazy Barrys. But this inanimate boy is not dressed in the comparatively modest attire of a troll or jockey. No, he wears a uniform that cries out, "Look at me!"; that says, "I'm Catholic and I'm proud"; that, in the case of this wispy specimen, mewls, "Please don't beat me up."

Retro-scavenging fashion designers take note, for this is what the boy wore: Green and gold, with a dash of flop-sweat. Dark green pants with a black stripe down the sides. Green socks. Green belt with gold trim. Black loafers sold exclusively by the shoe store near Ha-Cha Stationers up on Deer Park Avenue (a Catholic shakedown, his father muttered). A gold shirt with the circular icon of the Holy Spirit stitched into the breast pocket. A green tie emblazoned with the initials SCSM, which stood for the acutely sibilant name of his parish and parochial school: formally, St. Cyril and St. Methodius; casually, Saints Cyril and Methodius; finally, and most commonly, as though referring to a comedy duo with an occasional gig on the Ed Sullivan Show—Cyril and Methodius.

TOP

Andreas Feininger, Untitled [Autos on West Side Highway, today], c. 1950, gelatin silver print

The GI Bill and the construction of new suburbs on Long Island and in New Jersey helped pave the way for many Catholic families to leave the city in the post-World War II years.

BOTTOM

View of Levittown, New York, 1954

Built in Nassau County between 1947 and 1951, the planned community of Levittown was the first mass-produced suburb and a model for post-war suburban housing throughout the nation.

Dan Barry (second from left) on the occasion of his First Communion, with his parents, Gene and Noreen, and brother Brian outside their Deer Park, Long Island, home, 1966

Wearing this uniform, I knew that passing public-school bullies would feel duty-bound to dismount from their Sting-Rays and pummel me before continuing their commute to some truant endeavor. But I also knew that I was serving as a kind of green-and-gold billboard for my parents and other Roman Catholics who in recent years had moved from the apartments and tenements of New York City to the tract houses of Long Island. This billboard boy, and tens of thousands of uniformed children like him, proudly announced the formation of a new Catholic parish, a new Catholic diocese—a new way of defining a Catholic community.

Roman Catholics in New York City, as in just about every city in this country, lived in parishes, not neighborhoods. If, as newlyweds back in 1957, my parents were asked where they lived, they would not have said Jackson Heights, or even Queens. Their answer would have been, "St. Joan of Arc," a response that would have been as specific as any global positioning system. It would have provided a sense of place, of median income, even of ethnicity. In the crowded concrete corners of Manhattan and Queens, of Brooklyn and the Bronx, parishes were blocks away, not miles away, and in some cases you knew that this church was for the Italians in the neighborhood, this one for the Irish, this one for the Germans, this one for the Poles.

Things changed, though, when the likes of Gene and Noreen Barry left St. Joan of Arc for a place called Deer Park, 30 miles to the east and therefore in the country, in a place called Suffolk County, far beyond the last stop on the elevated subway line looming over Roosevelt Avenue. Where once there grew only scrub pines along the lonely Ronkonkoma line of the Long Island Rail Road, there now sprouted houses by the hundreds, by the thousands, filling with young married couples eager to settle down after spending their childhoods in the Depression and their young adulthoods at war. So many Catholics were moving to the Island that they outpaced the Church's ability to meet their needs; some of them had little choice but to celebrate Mass in vacant storefronts, movie theaters, firehouses—any place where they could gather in Jesus' name.

Finally, in early 1957, the Church announced the creation of a new diocese, the Diocese of Rockville Centre, to serve the nearly 500,000 Catholics now living in the Long Island counties of Nassau and Suffolk—a service that would include driving lessons for people accustomed to the New York City transit system (neither of my parents knew how to drive when they moved to Long Island). Alas, this new diocese was carved from the Diocese of Brooklyn, which would also suffer another loss both physical and spiritual in 1957, that of its beloved Dodgers.

By 1960, so many New York City Catholics had moved to Deer Park that the clapboard St. Cyril and St. Methodius Chapel, built in 1949 with what in hindsight proved to be a flawed analysis of population growth, was now barely large enough to serve as a crying room—or, in the vernacular of the time, "a mothers' room."

One summery day in 1963, His Excellency, Walter P. Kellenberg, the first bishop of Rockville Centre, resplendent in a gold miter, white gloves, and red-and-gold robes, came to Deer Park. He was launching so many fund raising events for new parish churches and buildings by this point that he joked posterity would remember to him as "Kick-off Kellenberg." And here he was, a vision on Deer Park Avenue, blessing the brand-new St. Cyril and St. Methodius Church: a cavernous cross-shaped structure with terrazzo floors, mosaic-tiled Stations of the Cross, and massive windows that on sunny days sprinkled congregants with stained-glass dapples of red and blue. The upper church's capacity of 1,200, though, was still not enough to meet the demand, so at least twice on Sunday mornings a portable altar was set up in the basement. Though this gray, dusky space received no stained-glass blessings, it did, at least, have a crying room.

Now, sitting beside one another in the pews upstairs and in the folding chairs downstairs, were Noreen and Gene Barry, formerly of St. Joan of Arc in Queens, and Bob and Anne Hornik, formerly of St. Simon Stock in the Bronx; John and Jeanne McShane, formerly of Our Lady of Perpetual Help, and Jim and June Sutton, formerly of St. Theresa's; the Seiberts and the Amatos and the Carews, shooshing toddlers who would soon be wearing green and gold at the new parochial school next door.

Thus I became part of the first wave to suffer taunts and fists for the greater glory of my parish and school, St. Cyril and St. Methodius. Some might say I was a loser; I like to think of myself as a martyr, albeit one who was never technically eviscerated or beheaded. In those green pants and that green tie, I presented myself to the world as someone committed to a community centered on a shared belief. If a couple of public-school knuckleheads stole the Wonder Bread bag containing my lunch—a balled-up peanut-butter sandwich and a couple of ShopRite cookies not worthy to share a cookie jar with a purebred Oreo—then I starved in the name of Jesus, Cyril, and Methodius—the Tinker, Evers, and Chance of my spiritual infield.

A suffering continued inside the school as well, and I do not necessarily mean at the hands of the Sisters of St. Joseph. I can tell "nun stories" with the best of them, but in truth the sisters who taught me reflected all parts of the human jumble: Some nurtured me with love, some tortured me with cruelty, and some were just there, gliding down dim corridors like small, black hovercraft.

The suffering came in other ways. Public-school children had playgrounds and jungle gyms; we had a parking lot and a Spaulding. They had gymnasiums, with basketball hoops and climbing ropes; we had a church basement, available for dodge ball only when it wasn't being used for Mass, bingo, lunch, or a school assembly. They had musical instruments and band; we had one class a semester in which we had to stand up in front of the class and sing.

In the fifth grade, the prospect of singing in front of my peers, in front of *girls*, in front of Kathleen Cudahy (!), whose glinting retainer dazzles still in memory, terrified me so much that I developed a fit of hysterical laughter. My teacher directed me to the back of the room and instructed the other students to train their eyes on the blank blackboard in front; in other words, DO NOT LOOK AT DANIEL WHILE HE SINGS. Four dozen sets of shoulders flinched at the sound of my first words to "My Country, Tis of Thee," including those of the lovely Kathleen Cudahy.

I spent eight years in green and gold, eight years that included Confession, First Holy Communion, Confirmation, and dozens of First Friday Masses. I played on the seventh-grade traveling basketball team for St. Cyril and St. Methodius, and scored two points the entire season. I played on the eighth-grade traveling baseball team, and got two hits. After graduating from the parochial school, I returned every Thursday night to work as a waiter during the bingo games in the church basement; one night the power went out, but the glow of votive candles allowed the calls to continue, chantlike, into the night, B-4, N-32, O-66….

And, of course, my family and I attended Sunday Mass, though usually in the basement for the 11:45, because the 11:30 High Mass upstairs was just a bit too early and a bit too much. But even in that subterranean haven, that place of dodge balls and bingo calls, we belonged.

Thirty years have passed since I went off to St. Bonaventure University in far-off Olean, N.Y., leaving Saints Cyril and Methodius and the Diocese of Rockville Centre behind. So much has changed since that boy with an overbite emerged from his house, wearing colors of green and gold.

The diocese has tripled since 1957, to 1.5 million Catholics—though the number of them regularly attending Mass falls far below even half that. It has triumphed in some ways, failed in others. There is its impressive expansion of programs for the ill and disenfranchised, and there is its egregious mishandling of cases of sexually predatory priests within its ranks.

Still, even now, even while living in another state, I consider St. Cyril and St. Methodius parish of the Diocese of Rockville Centre to be where I'm from. This sense has intensified in recent years, as I have returned several times to sit in one of its pews and receive again its stained-glass sprinkle of a blessing. The occasions have all been for the funerals of pioneers—my mother, for one—who long ago dressed their children in green and gold as a way to say, simply: We're here.

Walter P. Kellenberg, first bishop of the Diocese of
Rockville Centre, at St. Cyril and St. Methodius Roman
Catholic Church in Deer Park, c. 1968

TYLER ANBINDER is Professor of History at George Washington University and is the author of *Five Points: The 19th-Century New York City Neighborhood That Invented Tap Dance, Stole Elections, and Became the World's Most Notorious Slum* (New York: Free Press, 2001).

DAVID A. BADILLO is Associate Professor of Latin American and Puerto Rican Studies at Lehman College in the Bronx. His essay in this volume is adapted from his book, *Latinos and the New Immigrant Church* (Johns Hopkins University Press, 2006).

DAN BARRY writes a national column, "This Land," for *The New York Times;* he has also written a memoir, *Pull Me Up* (W.W. Norton & Company, 2004).

MARY ELIZABETH BROWN is Assistant Professor in the Social Science Division of Marymount Manhattan College and also assists with special projects at the Center for Migration Studies.

WILLIAM A. DONOHUE is President of the Catholic League for Religious and Civil Rights.

JAMES T. FISHER is Co-Director of the Francis and Ann Curran Center for American Catholic Studies at Fordham University.

DAVID GIBSON has written about Catholicism for periodicals including *The New York Times, The Wall Street Journal, New York* magazine, and *America,* and is the author of *The Coming Catholic Church: How the Faithful Are Shaping a New American Catholicism* (Harper-Collins, 2003). He has also worked for Vatican Radio in Rome, and has co-written several CNN documentaries on Christianity.

TERRY GOLWAY is a Kean University historian and journalist who has written for *The New York Times, American Heritage,* and the *New York Observer.* His publications include *Washington's General: Nathanael Greene and the Triumph of the American Revolution* (Henry Holt, 2006). He also edited the PBS series companion volume *The Irish in America* (Hyperion, 1997).

PETE HAMILL is a Brooklyn-born novelist, essayist, and journalist, and a Distinguished Writer in Residence at New York University. He has authored numerous books including *Snow in August* (Grand Central Publishing, 1998) and *A Drinking Life* (Back Bay Books, 1995), both of which were *New York Times* bestsellers; his most recent novel is *North River* (Little, Brown & Company, 2007).

JAMES THOMAS KEANE, S.J. is Associate Editor at *America* magazine and a scholastic of the Society of Jesus, preparing for ordination to the Roman Catholic priesthood.

SALVATORE J. LaGUMINA is a Professor of History at Nassau Community College and author of numerous articles and books on the Italian-American experience in New York City.

BERNADETTE McCAULEY is Associate Professor of History at Hunter College in Manhattan. She is the author of *Who Shall Take Care of Our Sick?* (Johns Hopkins University Press, 2005).

PATRICK J. McNAMARA has been Assistant Archivist at the Diocese of Brooklyn since 2000. He is the author of *A Catholic Cold War: Edmund Walsh, S.J., and the Politics of American Anticommunism* (Fordham University Press, 2005) and co-author of a history of the Brooklyn Diocese, *Diocese of Immigrants* (2004). He teaches history at St. Francis College, Brooklyn, and historical theology at the Seminary of the Immaculate Conception, Huntington, New York.

C. BRID NICHOLSON is Associate Professor of History at Kean University in Union Township, New Jersey.

EDWARD T. O'DONNELL is Associate Professor of History at the College of the Holy Cross in Worcester, Massachusetts. He is the author of *Ship Ablaze: The Tragedy of the Steamboat General Slocum* (Random House, 2003) and a forthcoming social biography of Henry George.

PETER QUINN, a third-generation New Yorker, is author of the novels *Banished Children of Eve* (Penguin Group, 1994) and *Hour of the Cat* (Overlook Press, 2005). He has worked as Executive Director for Time Warner and as a speechwriter for two New York governors. His essay in this volume is excerpted from his book, *Looking for Jimmy: A Search for Irish America* (Overlook Press, 2007).

ALEX STOROZYNSKI won a Pulitzer Prize for editorial writing as a member of the *New York Daily News* editorial board in 1999. He currently writes for the *New York Sun,* among other publications, and is working on a biography of Thaddeus Kosciuszko.

DEBORAH DEPENDAHL WATERS is Senior Curator, Decorative Arts and Manuscripts, Museum of the City of New York, and curator of its exhibition *Catholics in New York, 1808–1946.* She acted as curatorial coordinator for the Museum's exhibition *Gaelic Gotham* (1996).

IMAGE CREDITS

PAGE 10
Museum of the City of New York, J. Clarence Davies Collection, 29.100.792

PAGE 12
TOP LEFT: Museum of the City of New York, Museum purchase, 76.79; photograph by John Parnell
TOP RIGHT: Private collection; photograph by Ali Elai, Camerarts
BOTTOM LEFT: Courtesy of Fordham University Library Archives and Special Collections
BOTTOM RIGHT: © CORBIS (BK001064)

PAGE 15
TOP: © Bettmann/CORBIS (U307447INP)
BOTTOM: Courtesy of the Roman Catholic Diocese of Brooklyn

PAGES 16–17
Courtesy of the Roman Catholic Diocese of Brooklyn

PAGE 19
TOP LEFT: Courtesy of Elizabeth W. Colbert
TOP RIGHT: Courtesy of the Russo Family
BOTTOM: Justo A. Martí Photographic Collection, Archive of the Puerto Rican Diaspora, Centro de Estudios Puertorriqueños, Hunter College, CUNY

PAGE 22
Courtesy of Pete Hamill

PAGE 26
Museum of the City of New York, gift of the artist, 96.190

PAGE 29
TOP: Museum of the City of New York, Persson Collection, 97.167.1
BOTTOM LEFT: Museum of the City of New York, *Harper's Weekly* Collection
BOTTOM RIGHT: Museum of the City of New York, Byron Collection, 93.1.1.3170

PAGE 30
TOP: Courtesy of the Center For Migration Studies of New York, Inc.
BOTTOM: Museum of the City of New York, gift of Grace La Gambina, 92.40.5

PAGE 32
Museum of the City of New York, gift of Otto G. Klosinski, 37.291

PAGE 33
Museum of the City of New York, Jacob Riis Collection, 90.12.1.271

PAGE 35
TOP LEFT: Courtesy of the Center For Migration Studies of New York, Inc.
TOP RIGHT: Courtesy of the Center For Migration Studies of New York, Inc.
BOTTOM: Courtesy of Larry Racioppo

PAGE 36
Museum of the City of New York, gift of the artist, 96.190

PAGE 39
TOP: © Bettmann/CORBIS (BE027052)
BOTTOM LEFT: Library of Congress, Prints and Photographs Division (LC-USW3-014490-D)
BOTTOM RIGHT: Courtesy of the Brooklyn Historical Society

PAGE 40
Courtesy of the Brooklyn Public Library, Brooklyn Collection

PAGE 43
ALL IMAGES: Courtesy of the Roman Catholic Diocese of Brooklyn

PAGE 44
ALL IMAGES: Courtesy of the Roman Catholic Diocese of Brooklyn

PAGES 46–47
Courtesy of the Roman Catholic Diocese of Brooklyn

PAGE 50
ALL IMAGES: Courtesy of the Roman Catholic Diocese of Brooklyn

PAGE 53
ALL IMAGES: Courtesy of the Roman Catholic Diocese of Brooklyn

PAGE 54
Courtesy of Tamiment Library, New York University; photograph by Ali Elai, Camerarts

PAGE 57
TOP: © Bettmann/CORBIS (S1714)
BOTTOM: Courtesy of the Fenimore Art Museum, Cooperstown, New York; photograph by Richard Walker

PAGES 58–59
Museum of the City of New York, gift of Mrs. Robert M. Littlejohn, 33.169.1

PAGE 60
LEFT: Museum of the City of New York, gift of Mr. Gerald LeVino, 57.100.13
RIGHT: Museum of the City of New York, gift of Harry Shaw Newman, 46.415

PAGE 63
Museum of the City of New York, gift of Hobart Ford from the Simeon Ford Collection

PAGE 64
TOP: Library of Congress, Prints and Photographs Division (LC-USZC4-7964)
BOTTOM LEFT: Museum of the City of New York, gift of Gladys Hatos Zurkow, 95.147.20
BOTTOM RIGHT: Museum of the City of New York, Print Archives

PAGE 67
LEFT: Courtesy of the Archdiocese of New York; photograph by David Arky
TOP RIGHT: Museum of the City of New York, gift of Donald Greenhaus, 80.65.5; © Estate of Donald Greenhaus/Artists Rights Society (ARS), New York
BOTTOM RIGHT: James Estrin/The New York Times/Redux

PAGE 68
© Bettmann/CORBIS (BE046157)

PAGE 71
TOP: © Owen Franken/CORBIS (OF011192)
BOTTOM: © Bettmann/CORBIS (BE046157)

PAGE 72
TOP LEFT: Private Collection
TOP RIGHT: Courtesy of Tamiment Library, New York University; photograph by Ali Elai, Camerarts
BOTTOM: Courtesy of the Roman Catholic Diocese of Brooklyn

PAGE 74
TOP: Courtesy of the Roman Catholic Diocese of Brooklyn
BOTTOM: Courtesy of Dr. Joseph Wieczerzak

PAGE 75
TOP: Courtesy of the Polish American Collection, Immigration History Research Center, University of Minnesota (http://www1.umn.edu/ihrc/index.htm)
BOTTOM: Courtesy of Dr. Joseph Wieczerzak

PAGE 77
TOP: Courtesy of W. H. Sadlier, Inc.
BOTTOM: Museum of the City of New York, gift of Marguerite Lavin, 95.154; photograph by Ali Elai, Camerarts

PAGE 80
Courtesy of Sr. Mary Louise Sullivan, M.S.C., Cabriniana Room, Holy Spirit Library, Cabrini College, Radnor, PA 19087

PAGE 82
Courtesy of Emigrant Savings Bank

PAGE 85

TOP LEFT: Library of Congress, Prints and Photographs Division (LC-USZ62-105528)

TOP RIGHT: Private collection

BOTTOM: Museum of the City of New York, gift of Bella C. Landauer, 34.80.160A

PAGE 87

TOP: Courtesy of the General Research Division, The New York Public Library, Astor, Lenox and Tilden Foundations

BOTTOM: Museum of the City of New York, gift of Harry Shaw Newman, 54.369.2

PAGE 88

TOP LEFT: Courtesy of Emigrant Savings Bank

TOP RIGHT: Museum of the City of New York, Irving Underhill Collection, B.19848

BOTTOM: Courtesy of Emigrant Savings Bank

PAGES 90–91

Museum of the City of New York, gift of Lou Sepersky and Leida Snow

PAGE 94

Private collection

PAGE 96

Museum of the City of New York, Museum purchase, 95.54.12

PAGE 97

Private collection; photograph by Ali Elai, Camerarts

PAGE 99

TOP: Museum of the City of New York, Jacob Riis Collection #94, 90.12.1.97

LEFT: Museum of the City of New York, gift of the photographer

PAGE 100

TOP: Museum of the City of New York, Byron Collection, 93.1.1.5008

BOTTOM LEFT: Museum of the City of New York, Print Archives

BOTTOM RIGHT: Museum of the City of New York, Print Archives

PAGE 102

ALL IMAGES: Courtesy of Convent of the Sacred Heart

PAGE 103

© Joseph Schwartz/CORBIS (TZ001162)

PAGE 105

TOP: Museum of the City of New York, Byron Collection, 93.1.1.5104

BOTTOM: Museum of the City of New York, gift of the N.Y.C. WPA Art Project, 43.129.10

PAGE 107

© Bettmann/CORBIS (U1072838)

PAGE 108

Courtesy of the Rev. John LaFarge, S.J. Papers, Georgetown University Library, Special Collections Research Center, Washington, D.C.

PAGE 111

TOP: Courtesy of the Rev. John LaFarge, S.J. Papers, Box #65 Folder #1, Georgetown University Library, Special Collections Research Center, Washington, D.C.

BOTTOM: Courtesy of the Rev. John LaFarge, S.J. Papers, Box #65 Folder #2, Georgetown University Library, Special Collections Research Center, Washington, D.C.

PAGES 112–113

Courtesy of the Rev. John LaFarge, S.J. Papers, Box #65 Folder #7, Georgetown University Library, Special Collections Research Center, Washington, D.C.

PAGE 117

TOP: Courtesy of the American Catholic History Research Center and University Archives, The Catholic University of America, Washington, D.C.

BOTTOM LEFT: Courtesy of the American Catholic History Research Center and University Archives, The Catholic University of America, Washington, D.C.

BOTTOM RIGHT: Courtesy of the Rev. John LaFarge, S.J. Papers, Georgetown University Library, Special Collections Research Center, Washington, D.C.

PAGE 118

Museum of the City of New York, J. Clarence Davies Collection, 29.100.2297

PAGE 119

Courtesy of The New-York Historical Society, gift of Miss Georgina Schuyler

PAGE 120

TOP: Courtesy of Columbia University, Columbiana Collection

MIDDLE: Courtesy of the National Portrait Gallery, Smithsonian Institution; gift of Mr. and Mrs. Paul Mellon

BOTTOM: © Bettmann/CORBIS (U567651INP)

PAGE 121

ALL IMAGES: Courtesy of Tamiment Library, New York University; photograph by Ali Elai, Camerarts

PAGE 122

TOP: Courtesy of the Missionary Sisters of the Sacred Heart of Jesus

BOTTOM: © Hulton-Deutsch Collection/CORBIS (HU016459)

PAGE 123

TOP: © Bettmann/CORBIS (BE064360)

BOTTOM: Courtesy of the Marquette University Archives

PAGES 124–125

Museum of the City of New York, gift of the family of Governor Alfred E. Smith, 45.117.260

PAGE 126

Courtesy of Peter Quinn

PAGE 132

Museum of the City of New York, gift of Ilona Albok Parker, 82.68.27

PAGE 135

TOP: Private collection

BOTTOM LEFT: Museum of the City of New York, Print Archives

BOTTOM RIGHT: Museum of the City of New York, gift of the family of Governor Alfred E. Smith, 45.117.260

PAGE 136

Museum of the City of New York, 33.124

PAGE 137

TOP: Museum of the City of New York, Manuscript and Ephemera Collection

BOTTOM: Museum of the City of New York, gift of Joseph Brennan, 36.196.1, .2

PAGE 138

LEFT: Museum of the City of New York, gift of the estate of Joseph Morris Alexander, Receipt 324329-41

RIGHT TOP: Museum of the City of New York, gift of W. R. Grace & Co.

RIGHT MIDDLE: Museum of the City of New York, Byron Collection, 93.1.1.8725

RIGHT BOTTOM: Museum of the City of New York, Portrait Archives

PAGE 141

TOP LEFT: Museum of the City of New York, gift of the Family of Governor Alfred E. Smith, 45.117.33; photograph by Ali Elai, Camerarts

TOP RIGHT: Museum of the City of New York, gift of the Family of Governor Alfred E. Smith, 45.117.89, A 0050, 1928; photograph by Ali Elai, Camerarts

BOTTOM: Museum of the City of New York, gift of the Family of Governor Alfred E. Smith, 45.117.178

PAGE 142

TOP: Museum of the City of New York, Print Archives, gift of the artist

BOTTOM LEFT: Museum of the City of New York, gift of Ilona Albok Parker, 82.68.27

BOTTOM RIGHT: George Grantham Bain Collection, Library of Congress, Prints and Photographs Division (LC-USZ62-48852)

PAGE 144

TOP: Courtesy of the Collections of the Municipal Archives of the City of New York

BOTTOM: Museum of the City of New York, 89.49.1

PAGE 146

From Sylvester L. Malone, *Dr. Edward McGlynn* (New York: Dr. McGlynn Monument Association, 1918), between pp. 8–9

PAGE 149

TOP LEFT: Courtesy of Tamiment Library, New York University; photograph by Ali Elai, Camerarts

TOP RIGHT: Courtesy of Tamiment Library, New York University; photograph by Ali Elai, Camerarts

BOTTOM: Museum of the City of New York, J. Clarence Davies Collection, 29.100.13B; photograph Ali Elai, Camerarts

PAGE 150

TOP: Courtesy of Robert F. Wagner Labor Archives, Tamiment Library, New York University

BOTTOM: Courtesy of the Picture Collection, The Branch Libraries, The New York Public Library, Astor, Lenox and Tilden Foundations

PAGES 152–153

Courtesy of Sam Thomas

PAGE 155

TOP: Museum of the City of New York, 32.153.8 and 43.118.7; photograph by Ali Elai, Camerarts

BOTTOM LEFT: Museum of the City of New York, 36.177.64; photograph by Ali Elai, Camerarts

BOTTOM RIGHT: Courtesy of the Science, Industry & Business Library, The New York Public Library, Astor, Lenox and Tilden Foundations

PAGE 156

TOP LEFT: From Anna George de Mille, *Henry George Citizen of the World* (Chapel Hill: The University of North Carolina Press, 1950), between pp. 220–221

TOP RIGHT: From Sylvester L. Malone, *Dr. Edward McGlynn* (New York: Dr. McGlynn Monument Association 1918), between pp. 28–29

BOTTOM: From Anna George de Mille, *Henry George Citizen of the World* (Chapel Hill: The University of North Carolina Press, 1950), between pp 220–221

PAGE 161

From Sylvester L. Malone, *Dr. Edward McGlynn* (New York: Dr. McGlynn Monument Association 1918), between pp. 104–105

PAGE 162

Museum of the City of New York, gift of Grace M. Mayer, 92.50.132

PAGE 165

TOP: Museum of the City of New York, Print Archives

BOTTOM LEFT: Museum of the City of New York

BOTTOM RIGHT: Museum of the City of New York, gift of Grace M. Mayer, 92.50.132

PAGE 166

TOP LEFT: Museum of the City of New York, gift of the Federal Art Project, Work Projects Administration, 43.131.8.37

TOP RIGHT: Museum of the City of New York, purchase with funds from the Mrs. Elon H. Hooker Acquisition Fund, 40.140.53

BOTTOM: George Grantham Bain Collection, Library of Congress, Prints and Photographs Division (LC-USZ62-49242)

PAGE 169

TOP LEFT: Courtesy of Fordham University Library Archives and Special Collections

TOP MIDDLE: Private Collection

TOP RIGHT: Library of Congress, Prints and Photographs Division (LC-USZ62-19548)

BOTTOM: Photo by Keystone/Getty Images; courtesy of Getty Images

PAGE 173

Museum of the City of New York, Theater Archives

PAGE 176

Courtesy of William Donohue

PAGE 180

Courtesy of the Felipe N. Torres Papers, Archives of the Puerto Rican Diaspora, Centro de Estudios Puertorrique-ños, Hunter College, CUNY

PAGE 183

TOP: Museum of the City of New York, gift of Joseph Battle, 96.85.21

BOTTOM: Photo by H. Armstrong Roberts/Retrofile/Getty Images; courtesy of Getty Images

PAGE 187

ALL IMAGES: Courtesy of the Felipe N. Torres Papers, Archives of the Puerto Rican Diaspora, Centro de Estudios Puertorriqueños, Hunter College, CUNY

PAGE 188

© Bettmann/CORBIS (BE044768)

PAGE 190

TOP: Museum of the City of New York, gift of the photographer, 55.31.161

BOTTOM: © Bettmann/CORBIS (BE044768)

PAGE 191

Courtesy of Dan Barry

PAGE 195

Courtesy of Dan Barry

A

A Tree Grows in Brooklyn (Smith)   45

Academy of Music   158

African Americans   18, *44*, 48, 101, 110 passim, 119, 167, 177–178

America   18, 110, 115

American Federation of Labor   172

Angel Gabriel riots   42

anti-Catholicism – *See also* nativism   11–*12*, 17, 139, 159

anti-communism   116

Anti-Poverty Society   *156*, 158

Archdiocese of New York – Catholic Charities   37

Archdiocese of New York – Office of Catholic Action   184

Archdiocese of Newark   172

architecture   28, 56

Armenians   48

Association of Catholic Trade Unions   170

Awful Disclosures of the Hotel Dieu Nunnery   101

B

Baltimore Catechism   129

Bandini, Pietro   34

Barat Day Nursey   *102*

Batterham, Forster   123

Bealin, John   157

Bedford-Stuyvesant   42, *44*, 48

Belfast United   24

Bishops' Committee for the Spanish-Speaking   181

Bi-State Waterfront Commission   171

Bleecker Savings Bank   84, 86

Boston Christian Register   45

Bowery Savings Bank   84

Brando, Marlon   172–*173*

Brennan, Matthew T.   *137*, 139

Brooklyn Civic Center   182

Brooklyn Diocese – *See* Diocese of Brooklyn

Brooklyn Dodgers   192

Brooklyn Eagle   41–42, 48

Brooklyn Navy Yard   48, 182

Brooklyn Tablet   49–*50*, 52

Brooklyn-Queens Expressway   49

Burroughs, William S.   65

C

Cabrini, Frances Xavier   80–81, 101, *122*–123

The Call   123

Campanella, Roy   24

Cardinal Gibbons Institute   110, 114

Carey, Philip, S.J.   170

Cathedral High School   *15*

Catholic Action movement   114

Catholic Charities   37, 45

Catholic Interracial Council of New York   114 ff

The Catholic Publication Society   121

Catholic Review   45

Catholic Rural Life Movement   110

Catholic Seaman's Mission   65

Catholic University of Ponce   185–186

The Catholic Worker   51, 121, 123

Catholic Worker Movement   123, 170

Catholic Youth Organization (CYO)   18

Central Labor Union   154

Chelsea   164

Chelsea Piers   166

churches – *See* parishes or individual church name

City College – *See* Free Academy

Civil War   45, 61, *63*–*64*, 70, 84, 101, 104, 148

Claretian Missionaries   123

Collier's   95

Colored Catholic Club   48

Columbus Hospital   34, 37, 81

Columbus Press   122

Coman, Thomas   *137*

communism   51, 114, 116, 134, 143, 154, 170

Communist Party   18, 116, 128, 133, *142*–143, 159

Coney Island   *50*

Connolly, Joseph F.   184

Connolly, Richard B.   139

Convent of the Sacred Heart school   *102*

Corpus Christi procession   16

Corridan, John M.   170–171, 173

Corrigan, Michael Augustine   31 passim, 76, 122, 130, 154 passim

Coughlin, Charles   51

Croker, Richard   *138*

Cross-Bronx Expressway   182

Croton Aqueduct   134

D

Davis, Thurston N.   115

Davitt, Michael   151

Day, Dorothy   14, 17–18, 51, *123*

de Gaultier, Felisa Rincon   *187*

De Sapio, Carmine   143

Demo, Antonio   *35*, 38

Democratic Party   127 ff, 134 ff, 160, *187*

Diocese of Brooklyn   17, 28, 41 ff, 73, 95, 119, 185–186, 192

Diocese of Rockville Centre   52, 192, *195 (caption)*

Docks – *See* waterfront

Dominican Sisters   98

draft riots (1863)   *64*, 114, 164

Dry Dock District – *See* East Village

Dry Dock Savings Bank   84

DuBourg, William   120

Dunphy, James   *137*

E

East Harlem   18, *30*–31, 134, 182–*183*

East New York   51, 73

East River Savings Bank   84

East Village   18, 56, 62, 66

Ebbets Field   *46*–47

economy (New York City)   62

El Barrio   177–178, 182–*183*

Emigrant Savings Bank   17, 82 ff

Erie Canal   134

Esperanza parish   185

ethnic tensions   28–31, 34, 62, 66, 70, 73, 76, 133, 140, 168, 182

F

Farley, John Murphy   37

feast days   17, 28 ff

Felician Sisters   101

Ferrante, Gherardo   37

Ferraro, Geraldine   104

feste – *See* feast days

Fiesta of St. John the Baptist   184–185, *187*

Fifty-eighth New York Infantry Regiment   72 *(caption)*

First Vatican Council   135 *(caption)*

Fitzgibbon, Mary Irene   99

Five Points   88 *(caption)*, *90*–*91*, 92

Flynn, Ed   127, 130

Flynn, Elizabeth Gurley   18, 133, *142*, 159–160

Flynn, Thomas   159

Ford, John   129

Ford, Patrick   133, 151, 158

Fordham University   184

Fort Greene   73

Franciscan Handmaids of Mary   101

Free Academy (City College)   147

fundraising   45, 62, 73, 121, *137*, 193

G

Garibaldi statue, Washington Square   95, 143

George, Henry   148 passim

Georgetown University   185

German Redemptorist order   121

German Americans   14, 41 ff, 56, 70, 101, 121, 129, 133, 192

Gibbons, James   38

Ginsberg, Allen   65–66

Glackens, William   *94*–95, 106

Gompers, Samuel   61

Good Shepherd Sisters   98

Grace Institute   139

Grace, William R.   *138*–139

Graham, Isabella Marshall   120

Grand Knights of the Holy Sepulchre   170

Greenpoint   13, 73

Greenwich Village   28, 38, 66, 148, 164, 167
Guardian Angel parish   167
Gunther, John   51

H
Hague machine   127, 168
Hamill, Anne (*née* Devlin)   22 ff
Hamill, Billy   22 ff
Harlem   101
Hayes, Patrick Joseph   *15*, 37, 49
Heaney, Seamus   24
Hecker, George   121
Hecker, Isaac Thomas   109, 121–122
Hell's Kitchen   164, 167
Hijas de Maria   182
Hoboken   171
Hodges, Gil   52
Hodur, Father Franciszek   76
Holy Cross school   *74*
Holy Name parish   51
Holy Name school   24
Holy Name Society   44 passim, 134, 182
hospitals   17, 34, 37, 42, 81, 95, *99*–101, 104–*105*, 120, 122, 148, 182
Howard Beach   51
Hughes, Angela (Ellen)   *100 (caption)*
Hughes, John   *12*, 14, 17, *43 (caption)*, 56 passim, 76, 83, 98, *100 (caption)*–101, 121, 134, 139, 159

I
Illich, Ivan   185
immigration   11–13, 18, 27, 31, 56–*57*, 62, 65, 73, 101, 104, 139, *183 (caption)*
Impellitteri, Vincent   143–*144*
Index Librorum Prohibitorum   151
Industrial Liberator   151
Institute of Intercultural Communication (Catholic University of Ponce)   185
integrated (mixed) parishes   184
International Longshoremen's Association   167–*169*, 171
Interracial Justice: A Study of the Catholic Doctrine of Race Relations (LaFarge)   114
Ireland, John   52
Irish Americans   11, 14, 17, 24, 38, 41 ff, 56 ff, 73, 84 ff, 104, 129–130, 133 ff, 163 ff, 177–178, 182, 184, 192
Irish-American Catholics – economic conditions   61, 82 ff
Irish Emigrant Society   60, 83, *85*
Irish Land League   151, 154, 159
Irish World   133, 151
Italian Bureau   37
Italian Americans   24, 27 ff, 48, 51, 62, 65, 81, 104, 122, 129, 133, 140, 143, 167–168, 182, 192

Italian-American Catholics – immigration   27, 31, 38, 62, 65
Italian Auxiliary   37

J
Jack, Hulan   *187*
Jesuits   11–*12*, 18, 24, 109 passim, 122, *169*–171, 184
Jogues, Isaac   11–*12*
John Paul II   *68* ff, 123
John XXIII   115
Johnson, Malcolm   170–171

K
Keely, Patrick J.   *43 (caption)*, 56, 66
Kein, Richard   56, 61
Kellenberg, Walter P.   193, *195*
Kelly, John   139, 164
Kieft, William   11
King, Martin Luther, Jr.   115
Knights of Columbus   51, *53*
Knights of Malta   170
Knights of the Grand Cross   170
Know Nothings – *See* nativism
Kruszka, Waclaw   73, 76
Krzyzanowski, Wlodzimierz   70, 72
Ku Klux Klan   14, *50*, 51, 123

L
La Guardia, Fiorello H.   140
La Milagrosa parish   182
Labor Day parade   *150*
Labor schools   *169*, 170
Labor unions   24, 147 ff, *150*, 164 ff
LaFarge, John   18, 108 ff
Latino Catholics – *See* also Puerto Rican Catholics   14, 19, *44*, 48, 66, 181 ff
Lavelle, Michael Joseph   37
Leary, Annie
Leo XIII   27, 34, 122, 140, *152*–*153*, 157, 159
Levittown   *190*
Lincoln Center   184
Lincoln, Abraham   70
Lithuanians   48, 51
Little Germany   56
Long Island Railroad   192
longshoremen   163 ff
Loughlin, John   41 ff
Lower East Side   61, 65, 73, 122, 185
Loyalty Day parades   51
Lucey, Robert   181

M
Magrath, Philip J.   65
Malone, Sylvester   *41*–*43 (caption)*
The Manner Is Ordinary (LaFarge)   109
Marcantonio, Vito   17–18, 134, *142*
Maronites   48
Marymount   104
The Masses   123
Maurin, Peter   123
May, Michael   45
McCann, John H.   139
McCarthy, Joseph   51, 115
McCloskey, John   45, 73, 76, 121, 154, 164
McCormack, William J.   168 ff
McDonnell, Charles E.   45, 48–49, 73
McEntegart, Bryan J.   186
McGlynn, Edward   14, 146 ff
McGrath, Edward   51
McManus, James   185
McSweeney, Patrick   *57 (caption)*, 62 ff
Meehan, Thomas F.   48
Mielcuszny, Wojciech   70, 73
Missionaries of Saint Charles – *See* Scalabrinians
Missionary Institute of St. Charles Borremeo   122
Missionary Priests of St. Paul the Apostle – *See* Paulist Fathers
Missionary Sisters of the Sacred Heart of Jesus   81, 98, 104, *122*
missionaries   11–*12*, 34, 121–122, 129
Mitchel, John Purroy   133
Molloy, Thomas E.   *46*–47, 49, 52
Monk, Maria   *96*, 101
Mooney, Thomas   *60 (caption)*–62, 64
Moran, Michael   168
Morelli, Felix   34, 37
Moroni, Marcellino   34
Moses, Robert   140, 181, 184
Moskowitz, Belle   140
Most Holy Trinity parish   41, 45, 98
Most Precious Blood parish   34
Mundelein, George   45
Murphy, Charles Francis   17, *138*, 140

N
Napolitano, Carmine   48
Nast, Thomas   *135 (caption)*
National Catholic Conference on Interracial Justice   114, *117*
National Catholic Welfare Conference   37
national parishes   34, 38, *44 (caption)*, 48, 168, 181, 184
Native American Party   42, 134
nativism   13–14, 17, 42, 45, 134, 139, 148, 159
Nativity of the Blessed Virgin Mary   48

New Amsterdam *10–12 (caption)*
New York Catholics – population 11, 28, 41
New York Foundling Home *99–100,* 104
New York Freeman's Journal 76
New York State Crime Commission 170–171
New York Sun 170
The New York Times Magazine 171
Nuns – *See* women religious

O

O'Brien, Matthew 120
O'Connell, William H. 52
O'Connor, John 120
O'Donnell, John J. 167, 170
O'Dwyer, William O. 143–*144*
O'Hara, Frank 66
Old St. Patrick's 119–120
On the Waterfront 17, 171, 173
orphanages 17, 42, 45, 81, 95, *100,* 104, 119–120, 122
Orr, John S. 42
O'Toole, Peter 24
Our Lady of Czestochowa parish 73
Our Lady of Grace parish 51
Our Lady of Guadalupe parish 185
Our Lady of Lebanon Cathedral 48
Our Lady of Lourdes parish *53*
Our Lady of Mount Carmel parish 28, *30,* 182
Our Lady of Mount Carmel grotto 28, *35*
Our Lady of Monserrat chapel *19*
Our Lady of Peace nursery *15*
Our Lady of Perpetual Help parish 193
Our Lady of Pilar parish *44,* 48
Our Lady of Pompeii parish 28, *35 (caption),* 37–38, 122

P

parish identity 51 ff
parish life 17, 51, *53,* 55, 81, 186, 192
parishes:
    Esperanza 185
    Guardian Angel 167
    Holy Name 51
    La Milagrosa 182
    Most Holy Trinity 41, 45
    Most Precious Blood 34
    Our Lady of Czestochowa 73
    Our Lady of Grace 51
    Our Lady of Guadalupe 185
    Our Lady of Lourdes *53*
    Our Lady of Mount Carmel 28, *30,* 182
    Our Lady of Perpetual Help 193
    Our Lady of Pilar *44,* 48
    Our Lady of Pompeii 37
    Sacred Heart 164

St. Ann's (Brooklyn) 48
St. Ann's (Manhattan) 148
St. Anthony of Padua 28
St. Augustine 51
St. Brigid's 18, 54 ff, 148
St. Benedict the Moor (Queens) 48
St. Casimir's 73
St. Cyril and St. Methodius 189, 193–*195*
St. Fortunata's 51
St. Francis Xavier 51
St. George's 48
St. Ignatius Loyola 115
St. James's 148
St. Joachim 34, 37
St. Joan of Arc 192–193
St. John Cantius 51, 73
St. John the Baptist *42–43*
St. Lucy's 18
St. Malachy's 51
St. Mary Queen of the Isle 42
St. Mary's (Newburgh, New York) 159
St. Mary's (Southern Maryland) 110–*111*
St. Matthew's 184
St. Michael's *44,* 51
St. Peter's 119–120
St. Rita's 51
St. Rose of Lima 182
St. Saviour 51
St. Simon Stock 193
St. Stanislaus Kostka 73
St. Stephen's 147 ff
St. Theresa's 193
St. Veronica's 164
St. Vincent de Paul 119
Saints Joachim and Anne 49
Saints Peter and Paul 41–*43*
Transfiguration 34
parishes, Augustinian 185
parishes, Vincentian *42–43 (caption),* 185–186
Park Slope 51
Parmentier, Rosine 98
Paulist Fathers 109, 121
Paulist Press 122
Pecora, Ferdinand 143
Pennsylvania Railroad 168
Pentecostals 186
Perkins, Frances 140
Pius XI 114, 123
Polish Americans 13–14, 48, 51, 68 ff, 101, 167, 192
Polish Catholic Gazette 70
Polish National Catholic Church 76
Polish National Catholic Church of Resurrection 74–75
politics 17, 126 ff, 132 ff, 151

population 28, 41–42, 48–49, 56, 65, 70, 110, *183 (caption),* 186
Port of Elizabeth 172
Port of Newark 172
Preston, Monsignor Thomas 157
Progress and Poverty (George) 148 ff
protest *64 (caption),* 123, 147, 157–159
Protestants 11, 23–24, *43 (caption),* 121–122, 128–129, 139 ff, 163, 186
Public School Society 139
Puerto Rican Catholics 18, *44,* 48, 66, 177 ff
Pulaski Day 75

Q

Queens Village 49
Quinn, Bernard J. *44,* 48
Quinn, Peter A. *126* ff

R

The Race Question and the Negro (LaFarge) 115
radicalism 123, 147 ff, 170
Raffeiner, Johann 41
Raffeiner, Stephen 98
Randall's Island 185, *187*
Red Hook 42, 182
Redemptorists 121, 186
Regis High School 24
Religious of the Holy Union of the Sacred Hearts *99*
Religious of the Sacred Heart of Jesus *102*
Republican Party 129–130, 140–143, 157
Rerum Novarum 140, 159
Resurrection Chapel 34
Robinson, Jackie 24
Rockefeller, David *172*
Rockefeller, Nelson 172
Roman Catholic Orphan Asylum *100,* 119
Roosevelt, Franklin Delano 24, 127 ff
Roosevelt, Theodore 157
Rosebank (Staten Island) 28, *35*
Ryan, John A. 159
Ryan, Joseph P. 167 ff

S

Sacred Heart parish 164
Sacred Heart Sisters – *See* Missionary Sisters of the Sacred Heart of Jesus
St. Agnes Parochial School *107*
St. Ann's Armenian Cathedral 48
St. Ann's parish (Brooklyn) 48
St. Ann's parish (Manhattan) 148
St. Anthony of Padua 128
St. Anthony of Padua parish 28
St. Augustine parish 51

St. Benedict the Moor parish (Queens)   48
St. Bonaventure University   194
St. Bridget's – See St. Brigid's
St. Brigid's parish   54 ff, 148
St. Brigid's school   60, 67 (caption), 148
St. Casimir's parish   73
St. Cyril and St. Methodius parish   189, 193–195
St. Fortunata's parish   51
St. Francis de Sales school   99
St. Francis Hospital   105
St. Francis Xavier parish   51
St. George's parish   48
St. Ignatius Loyola parish   115
St. James Cathedral-Basilica   40, 48
St. James's parish   148
St. Joachim parish   34, 37
St. Joan of Arc parish   192–193
St. John Cantius parish   51, 73
St. John the Baptist parish   42–43
St. John's College   43 (caption)
St. Joseph Seminary   38
St. Lucy's parish   18
St. Lucy's school   18, 176–178
St. Malachy's parish   51
St. Mary Queen of the Isle parish   42
St. Mary's parish (Newburgh, New York)   159
St. Mary's parish (Southern Maryland)   110–111
St. Mary's Seminary   120
St. Matthew's parish   184
St. Michael's parish   44, 51
St. Patrick's Cathedral   56, 62–63, 118, 120, 174–175, 185
St. Patrick's Day parade   24
St. Peter Claver   44, 48
St. Peter's parish   119–120
St. Raphael Society for the Protection of Italian Immigrants   31 ff
St. Raymond's Grammar School   126, 130
St. Rita's parish   51
St. Rocco   32–33, 37, 39
St. Rose of Lima parish   182
St. Saviour parish   51
St. Simon Stock parish   193
St. Stanislaus Kostka school   72
St. Stanislaus Kostka parish   73
St. Stephen's parish   56, 146 ff
St. Theresa's parish   193
St. Veronica's parish   164
St. Vincent de Paul parish   119
St. Vincent's Hospital   100
Saint, Eva Marie   173
Saints Joachim and Anne parish   49
Saints Peter and Paul parish   41–43
Salve Regina   128

San Gennaro festival   30
San Rocco – See St. Rocco
Scalabrini, Giovanni Battista   31 ff, 122
Scalabrinians   35
Scanlan, Patrick   50 (caption)–51
schools   11, 61, 73, 104, 139, 148, 192 passim
schools:
    Cathedral   15
    Convent of the Sacred Heart   102
    Holy Cross   74
    Holy Name   24
    Regis   24
    St. Agnes   107
    St. Brigid's   60, 67 (caption), 148
    St. Francis de Sales   99
    St. Lucy's   18, 176–178
    St. Raymond's   126, 130
    St. Stanislaus Kostka   72
Schulberg, Budd   170–171
Schurz, Carl   70
Second Vatican Council   66
self-segregation   17, 73
Seton, Elizabeth Ann Bayley   14, 97 (caption)–98, 120–121
Sharp, John K.   73
Shea Stadium   71, 178
Shrine Church of the Sea   167
Simeoni, Cardinal   157
Sinn Fein   23
Sisters of Charity   60 (caption), 97 passim
Sisters of Charity of St. Joseph   120
Sisters of Mercy   98, 101
Sisters of St. Joseph   98, 101, 193
Sisters of the Poor of St. Francis   105
Sixpenny Savings Bank   84
Sixty-Ninth New York Regiment   61, 63–64
Smith, Alfred E., Jr.   17, 124–125, 130 ff, 168
Smith, Alfred E., Sr.   160
Smith, Betty   45
Sociedad del Santo Nombre (see Holy Name Society)   44, 182
Society for the Relief of Poor Widows with Small Children   120
South Brooklyn   73, 167, 182
Spanish Harlem   177–178, 183
Spanish Mass   19, 66, 182 ff
Spellman, Francis   49, 52, 134, 143, 167, 180 ff
Staten Island   13, 28, 35, 52, 123, 167
Stritch, Samuel   181
suburbanization   52, 76, 188 ff
Sullivan, Tim   143
Sweeney, Peter B.   139

T
The Tablet   49 ff
Tammany Hall   124–125, 127, 130, 134 ff, 147 ff, 164, 168
territorial parishes   38, 182, 184
Thérèse of Lisieux   48
Tobin, Austin J.   171–172
Tompkins Square Park   56, 64, 67
Torres, Felipe N.   187
Toussaint, Pierre   119–120
Transfiguration parish   34
Triborough Bridge   49
trusteeship controversy (schools)   76
Tweed, William M.   135 (caption)–136 (caption), 139, 164

U
Ukranians   51
Union Square   147, 150, 154
United Labor Party   154, 157, 159
Urban College of the Propaganda   147
Ursuline Sisters   98

V
Vincentians   42–43 (caption), 185–186

W
Warren and Wetmore architects   166–167
Washington Heights   182
Washington Square Park   94–95, 143
waterfront   17, 65, 163 ff
Webster Hall   23
West Village   164, 168
White, Bridget   83–84, 92
White, Richard   86, 92
Williamsburg   39, 41 ff, 98
Wilson, James J.   185
Windsor Terrace   24
Wodzicki, Piotr   73
Wojtyła, Karol - See John Paul II
women religious   15, 17, 42, 60, 81, 94 ff, 120, 122 (caption), 185, 193
workers   17, 62, 81, 89, 140, 150 (caption)–151, 164, 166, 169 (caption), 170
World Trade Center   172
World War I   38, 45, 48–49, 167–168
World War II   13, 18, 30 (caption), 76, 110, 123, 142 (caption), 181, 183 (caption), 190 (caption)

X
Xavier Labor School   169, 170

Y
Young Catholic   121
Yugoslavs   167